More Praise for *The Healing Practice* *of Celebration*

"Elaine Heath invites people of Christ to hear God's invitation to embody such a prayer as to meet our neighbors in the wildness of their lives. She has reminded us that it is exactly when we are dazed by fear, distress, confusion, and grief that God invites us to receive the victory of God's resurrection in a celebration of community. In a moment when the country is tempted to lean away from each other, Heath gives words to God's faithfulness and encourages us to lean in."
—C. Andrew Doyle, Episcopal Bishop, Diocese of Texas

"Elaine Heath delivers a deeply personal, vulnerable book that meets each of us in the very real places of our particular journeys while pointing us toward a hope-filled future through Christ. Elaine's wrestling with such topics as depression, failure, and societal tensions juxtaposed with God's presence, healing, and restoration could not come at a better time. *The Healing Practice of Celebration* provides engaging discourse coupled with practical questions for personal or corporate reflection. I plan to use this book with our small groups as well as a variety of other ministries as a tool for spiritual contemplation and engagement. This should be a must read for anyone responsible for the cultural development of their congregation or community."
—Douglas A. Hill, lead pastor, Abiding Hope Church, Littleton, CO

"She had me at the introduction. Anyone who can write a book on celebration and begin it with an honest conversation about grief, brokenness, and joylessness is speaking truth to a world that is dying for it. Heath shows how celebration is a spiritual discipline, both core to the Christian tradition and an instrument of healing. A fresh thought, necessary now more than ever before."
—Kathleen McShane, senior pastor, Los Altos United Methodist Church, Los Altos, CA

"Wow! This book responds to the need of the hour, begging to be read and internalized by every layperson, clergy, theologian, and ecclesiastical leader. It builds on a strong biblical foundation with challenging theological insights, concrete practical ideas, and inspiring questions to ponder."
—Sudarshana Devadhar, resident bishop, The United Methodist Church, Boston Area

"An insightful and inspiring book! Through scripture, history, and personal prose, Elaine Heath offers a powerful reimagining of the importance of the spiritual practice of celebration in the Christian life. Beyond festivity and merrymaking, this book exposes celebration's transformative power of healing as we find our bearings through the spiritual fog of failure and division. Permeating the text is Heath's gentle reminder that celebration, like all Christian practice, opens us to the reconciling love of God—becoming one with God, ourselves, and all creation."
—Josh R. Sweeden, dean of the faculty and associate professor of church and society, Nazarene Theological Seminary, Kansas City, MO

"The richness of this book cannot be contained in a brief endorsement. In it, Elaine expands celebration beyond a momentary response into an ongoing spiritual practice that can be experienced across life's full spectrum of thoughts and feelings. Rooted in scripture and tradition, Elaine brings celebration to life through her story and the stories of other. This book is a rare find and precious gift."
—Steve Harper, retired UMC elder and professor of spiritual formation; author, *Life in Christ*, from Abingdon Press

"What a hopeful, joyful book this is! Just as the antidote to despair is praise, here we discover how celebration is the antidote to disappointment, darkness, and disagreement. Elaine Heath lovingly and wisely shows us that celebration isn't dependent on feeling or circumstance and can be cultivated over time with God and others. A lovely gift for personal reflection and group study."
—James C. Howell, pastor, Myers Park United Methodist Church, Charlotte, NC; author, *Weak Enough to Lead*, from Abingdon Press

Elaine A. Heath

The Healing Practice *of* Celebration

Abingdon Press™
Nashville

Contents

Introduction

What comes to mind when you hear the word *celebrate*?
Do you imagine a birthday party with friends and
family, balloons, gifts, and a cake? Perhaps your first
thought is holidays such as Christmas or dinner out because you
got a raise in pay. There are religious celebrations, too, within the
liturgical year and in the sacraments. In most of these forms of
celebration there is joy because they are attached to experiences
that feel good.

But what does it mean for us to practice the spiritual discipline of celebration when we do not feel joyful, when we did
not get the raise we hoped for, when our son did not stop taking
drugs, when we lost our job, when the test results came back and
our world was turned upside down? While it might seem counterintuitive, the Christian practice of celebration is most potent and
most healing at times like these.

The central reason for Christian celebration is that God in
Christ is making all things new (Revelation 21:5). Jesus shows
us that God is for us and not against us. God is with us and not
absent. In Jesus, God "became flesh and blood, and moved into
the neighborhood" (John 1:14 MSG). God keeps moving into

the neighborhood of each of our lives and communities. We are not alone.

Having said all of that, this is the first time I have written a book that I absolutely did not want to write. I even tried to get out of it, but it was too late to do so.

I believe in the spiritual practice of celebration, to be sure. Celebration is an important part of the Christian life and central to the liturgical calendar. The sacraments of baptism and Holy Communion are celebrations that ground believers in the life, death, and resurrection of Jesus. My resistance had nothing to do with my beliefs about celebration. The fact was that months after I had agreed to write this book, when it was too late to change my mind, I was unable to write because I was depressed. I had no creative energy for anything. As anyone who has experienced depression knows, symptoms include emotional flatness, an inability to enjoy activities that are normally life-giving, disrupted sleep patterns, and apathy. Depression isn't the opposite of happiness. It is the opposite of feeling. And how could I write about celebration when I felt nothing except exhaustion?

My depression was what medical professionals refer to as "situational," caused by a convergence of extremely stressful events including my mother's death and the decision to leave my tenured faculty post. I was so numb from stress and exhaustion that when my mother died I was unable to cry or to feel anything. My body was so full of pain that at times it was difficult to walk. I took a sabbatical in order to help my body release the trauma it held.

I am profoundly grateful for the support of my husband, family, and friends and the homely chores of tending our small farm as I began to heal. The nonagricultural part of our land (Spring Forest) is a beautiful forest with soaring pines and hardwoods, pine-scented trails, abundant flora and fungi, and wildlife. Over the next few months my previous pace of seventy-hour work weeks gave way to forest walks, tending chickens, making soup, therapy, reading, and sleep. Spring slowly came to the farm after a long, cold winter. Finally, with the blooming of the redbuds and my mother's favorite, the dogwoods, my heart slowly opened to release the buried pain of loss. I began to feel again.

Grief is crazy-making. One day you have energy and creativity. You almost feel like yourself again, so you schedule a dinner party with friends for the following week. But when next week comes you can't bear to see or talk to anyone, much less hold a dinner party. Everything that used to seem solid now feels tentative, fragile, uncertain. You second-guess yourself about the smallest matters. You find yourself sitting in a chair staring into space wondering if you'll ever be yourself again.

It was on one of those hard days when the dogwoods were in bloom that I decided I was unable to write about celebration. But I realized that celebration was the spiritual practice that had kept me going through many hard days. Celebration was the spiritual discipline that was, even then, slowly bringing me back to life. Over the next many months, I wrote, section by section, and continued to heal. Today I am well. Writing this book was a significant part of what helped me to heal.

This book, then, is about the spiritual practice of Christian celebration, which is always focused on God making all things new (Revelation 21:5). Celebration is always bound to brokenness, loss, and lament. Just as the resurrected Jesus's promise to make all things new was spoken in the fiery apocalypse of Revelation, celebration bursts forth from us Christians in our personal cataclysms ushered in through a death, the loss of a job, the end of a relationship, or a dark night of the soul.

In the pages ahead we will visit narratives from the Bible and people in our own day who learned to celebrate in hard times because they trusted that God was making all things new. We will listen to their pain; marvel at their stories; find ourselves in their struggles with shame, fear, depression, trauma, and loss; and learn from their hard-won wisdom. We will do this so that we, too, can know and celebrate the wondrous goodness of God. No matter what.

Chapter One

Into the Wild

It is early in the morning at Spring Forest. The sun has risen, but its warmth does not penetrate the thick fog. Ghostly trees fade into the mist, edges softened in the damp stillness of the new day. I step outside. Though I cannot see birds, I hear morning songs of cardinals, blue jays, robins, flickers, crows. The scent of field and forest filling the air lets me know the world is much bigger and more alive than the fog suggests. Even so, the damp mist leaves on its own timetable. For now, I must live with the immediacy of hampered vision.

And so often this is what is required of us in life in the Spirit. We go about our workaday lives, loving and trusting God, then without warning a cold fog rolls in. Sometimes it comes through an illness. It can happen on the heels of a loss, a disappointment, a conflict, a betrayal. The fog can arrive when we lose our way spiritually and keep trying to justify ourselves to ourselves. At other times we simply do not know why it happens. We remember the blue skies of past experience with God. We recall the beauty and warmth of worship, the clarity of God's call to deeper faith. We remember feeling the joy of the Lord. But warmth, brightness, joy, and vision are only memories in the fog. What we now feel is loneliness and emptiness. And fear.

It was during one of those times many years ago that I first encountered Teresa of Ávila's poem "Let Nothing Disturb You." A Catholic friend came to see me in the hospital bearing a small, laminated prayer card with Teresa's picture on the front and the short poem on the back.[1] Pressing it into my palm, Karen said, "Trust me. This will help."

That day was in the middle of a painful, lengthy illness that included several hospitalizations and frustratingly inconclusive tests until the doctors were able to diagnose the disease and begin a treatment plan. I did not know how I would be able to finish seminary, much less answer God's call to ministry. Each day I had to take two or more naps due to the exhaustion of the illness. Because I needed long-term intravenous therapy, when I returned to seminary I had to take an IV pole with me to class and everywhere else, taking breaks when it was time for another infusion. But along with the IV pole, I carried the little prayer card with its potent, medicinal words:

Let nothing disturb you
Let nothing frighten you
All things are passing
God never changes

---

1. St. Teresa of Ávila (1515–1582) was a member of the Spanish nobility who chose a monastic life with the Carmelites. She was a notable reformer during the Counter-Reformation of the Roman Catholic Church among both male and female Carmelites, and one of the great Christian mystics of the church. She was declared a Doctor of the Church hundreds of years after her death because of the power and integrity of her theology and ministry. One of her most famous books, a classic in Christian spirituality, is *Interior Castle*. See Keith J. Egan, "Carmelite Spirituality," *The New Dictionary of Catholic Spirituality*, ed. Michael Downey (Collegeville, MN: Michael Glazer/The Liturgical Press, 1993), 117–25.

Patience obtains all things
She who possesses God lacks nothing
God alone suffices.[2]

Teresa's words echoed in my mind day by day, assuaging fear, urging patience, helping me lean into God as my sufficiency. It took three years to fully recover from the illness. Along the way I gained a deep compassion for people with chronic illness and a new perspective on "the God of the fog." Somehow the process even gave me needed detachment from my call to ministry so that my vocation could emerge from being God's beloved rather than from trying to prove my love for God. These gifts were given in no small part because Teresa (and Karen) helped me to celebrate the God who is present in fog, and the good future God promises, when celebration was the last thing I wanted to do.

And that is what the spiritual practice of celebration is all about. For Christians, the discipline of celebration focuses on God's deliverance from evil, liberation from bondage, healing of wounds, and forgiveness of sin. The word *salvation*, which sums up those four acts, is based upon a Latin word, *salve*, which means any remedy or action that heals. We celebrate as Christians because of God's wondrous gift of *salve* in Christ. We celebrate because Christ is making all things new, before we see the fullness of salvation happen. Salvation is for the whole world, to heal *all* things that have been broken by sin and evil. We celebrate the vast inclusiveness of salvation. Nothing will be wasted or lost. The apostle Paul described the magnitude of the *salve* of Christ

2. Teresa of Ávila's famous poem "Let Nothing Disturb You" is found in numerous places, including the home page for the Order of Carmelites, of which she was a member: http://ocarm.org/en/content/let-nothing-disturb-you.

in this way, repeating the word *all* seven times to make clear the comprehensiveness of salvation:

> He is the image of the invisible God, the firstborn of all creation; for in him all things in heaven and on earth were created, things visible and invisible, whether thrones or dominions or rulers or powers—all things have been created through him and for him. He himself is before all things, and in him all things hold together. He is the head of the body, the church; he is the beginning, the firstborn from the dead, so that he might come to have first place in everything. For in him all the fullness of God was pleased to dwell, and through him God was pleased to reconcile to himself all things, whether on earth or in heaven, by making peace through the blood of his cross. (Colossians 1:15-20)

Despite this beautiful declaration from the Bible, when we are in the fog such words can take on a feeling of unreality. Troubling thoughts tempt us to think that the God we once knew was only in our imagination. "The real God," temptation whispers, "doesn't care. Where is God? Gone. Just give up now." Such temptations come whether the fog is a result of poor choices on our part, deliberately harmful acts on the part of others, distressing circumstances, or a true dark night of the soul—an experience we will consider in a moment. Because of the pain of this kind of struggle, we need wisdom from faithful Christians who have gone before us, people like Teresa of Ávila. Their stories and teachings help us to know how to stand fast in faith when it seems as if God has disappeared.

Questions for Reflection

1. Have you ever experienced a "season of fog" in your faith journey? If so, how did you experience it? What were

the circumstances? Who companioned you through that experience? If you are on the other side of that experience now, how has it shaped your spiritual life?

2. The root meaning of *salvation* is "salve," any remedy or action that heals. How does this healing understanding of salvation compare to what you previously thought this word meant?

3. When we understand salvation as God's healing work, how might that change how we understand the mission of the church and our own individual paths of following Jesus?

4. The Christian discipline of celebration focuses on God's deliverance from evil, liberation from bondage, healing of wounds, and forgiveness of sin. Thus, celebration is always linked to situations of suffering, oppression, and brokenness in ourselves and in the world. We will explore the practice of celebration in depth in the pages ahead, but for now, what are some questions that arise as you consider the meaning of Christian celebration?

The Dark Night of the Soul[3]

The term *dark night of the soul* originated with John of the Cross, a close friend of Teresa of Ávila. John was the sixteenth-century Spanish Carmelite whose complex poem *Dark Night of*

---

3. A more scholarly version of this section is found in Elaine A. Heath, *The Mystic Way of Evangelism: A Contemplative Vision for Christian Outreach*, 2nd edition, revised and updated (Grand Rapids: Baker Academic, 2017). Excerpt from *The Mystic Way of Evangelism*, by Elaine Heath, copyright © 2008, 2017. Used by permission of Baker Academic, a division of Baker Publishing Group.

the Soul continues to resonate with Christians from many spiritual traditions. His poetry and theology have long attracted scholarly attention because of their depth and brilliance.[4] John defines different phases of the dark night in the life of faith. Most importantly, he describes the dark night as a God-initiated process that frees the soul from attachments that hinder the ability to receive and give God's love. For John, the dark night is not to be confused with depression (which he calls melancholia) or simply going through a rough time. Rather, it is an experience that God initiates to open wider space in us for love.

Three hundred years after John of the Cross wrote his stunning poem, nineteenth-century Welsh spiritual writer Jessie Penn-Lewis described the dark night using her own language and theological framework. The night is the time to surrender the "spiritually religious self," religious views, old ways, thought patterns, and activities that have become idolatrous substitutes for God in and of themselves. "If we surrender even the manifest presence of God, we become rooted and fixed in God. Not that He wants to take all away, but He wants us to surrender, that He might reveal himself as an abiding reality."[5]

4. For an introduction to the writings and a variety of contemporary reflections on John of the Cross, see John of the Cross, *Selected Writings*, Classics of Western Spirituality, ed. Kieran Kavanaugh and Ernest E. Larkin (New York: Paulist, 1987); Susan Muto, *John of the Cross for Today: The Dark Night* (Notre Dame, IN: Ave Maria Press, 1994); Hein Blommestijn et al., *The Footprints of Love: John of the Cross as Guide in the Wilderness*, trans. John Vriend (Louvain: Peeters, 2000); Francis Kelly Nemeck and Marie Theresa Coombs, *O Blessed Night* (New York: Alba House, 1991); and Gerald May, *The Dark Night of the Soul: A Psychiatrist Explores the Connection between Darkness and Spiritual Growth* (San Francisco: HarperSanFrancisco, 2004).

5. Jessie Penn-Lewis, *Fruitful Living* (Dorset, UK: Overcomer Literature Trust, n.d.), 19–20.

In the Bible we find many stories of God's people in the night. Sometimes in these narratives the night has to do with the apparent thwarting of the divine call or promise in an individual's life. We see this in Joseph's years of imprisonment in Egypt, Moses's decades as a shepherd, David's long years of exile during Saul's increasingly paranoid reign. The night is also revealed in God's people as they experienced the seeming absence of God during times of oppression or suffering. It is revealed in the barren yearning of Sarah, Leah, and Hannah; in Habakkuk's complaint; in Jeremiah's anguished cry; and in the mystery of Job's suffering. The dark night reaches its climax in the cry of Jesus on the cross: "My God, my God, why have you forsaken me?" (Matthew 27:46 NIV).[6]

The detachment brought about by the dark night, described by so many who have experienced it, is often from religious rigidity or from religious activity that has become in itself a god. This detachment takes place gradually, sometimes imperceptibly; at other times with great struggle and grief. Often those who are in the night are unaware of the nature of their attachments, especially religious attachments. Nicodemus, for example, sneaked out at night to question Jesus about the spiritual path. His attachment to the prestige and power of being a respected religious leader kept him from openly going to Jesus. What would his colleagues think?! His attachment to his own religious tradition also kept him from seeing the truth in front of him, though he found himself irresistibly drawn to Jesus (John 3:1-21).

6. Hans Urs von Balthasar sees Jesus's solidarity with humanity in such complete terms that the cry of Jesus on the cross, his experience of godforsakenness, and his descent into hell are all to be taken literally and seriously (Hans Urs von Balthasar, *Credo*, introduction by Medard Kehl, trans. David Kipp [New York: Crossroad,1990], 52).

In his book *The Dark Night of the Soul*, theologian and psychiatrist Gerald May notes, "Sometimes this letting go of old ways is painful, occasionally even devastating. But this is not why the night is called 'dark.' The darkness of the night implies nothing sinister, only that the liberation takes place in hidden ways, beneath our knowledge and understanding."[7] One of the clear signs of a dark night is its very obscurity, as if an opaque veil protects the cleansing, purifying work.

The cumulative effect of the dark night when embraced by God's people is the deconstruction of self-centeredness and the removal of subtle idolatry in terms of mistaking God for religious feeling and activity, or created things, or God as one more "thing." The dark night brings about a necessary detachment so that God's people may freely love all things in and through the love of God rather than in and of themselves. Religious activities, rituals, and practices especially are cleansed so that they are now, in the oft-quoted imagery of Thomas Merton, fingers pointing to the moon and no longer mistaken for the moon itself. The fruit of the night is about the transformation of relationships into expressions of love of God and neighbor and love of self for the sake of God.[8]

May is correct in his assessment that John of the Cross has often been misunderstood by subsequent interpreters, especially

---

7. May, *The Dark Night of the Soul*, 5.

8. Here, the insights of Bernard of Clairvaux (1090–1153) in his teaching on the "four degrees of love" are helpful. These are progressive, with the fourth and ultimate degree occurring only intermittently in this mortal life. The four degrees are: love of self for self's sake, love of God for self's sake, love of God for God's sake, and, finally, love of self for God's sake (Bernard of Clairvaux, "Four Degrees of Love," in *Invitation to Christian Spirituality*, ed. John R. Tyson [New York: Oxford University Press, 1999], 149–53).

when used to promote negative images of God.[9] For the "salve" of God is present and active in the night, bringing about growth, healing, and freedom, gifts of detachment from enmeshed relationships, compulsions, addictions, and idolatries that are not immediately apparent to those who have yet to emerge from the night.[10]

In some sense the emergence from the night is never complete in this life, for the process of God's leading to further growth and freedom is lifelong. It is part of the process of sanctification, of being made holy. Thus, we go through night seasons during which we experience detachment.

Language about detachment requires careful interpretation, especially when reading spiritual writings by John of the Cross and other great Christian mystics. Rather than being a process of complete separation from people and things we love (though at times it does mean separation), detachment in this context is best understood as the transformation of one's relationships with self, others, the created world, and God, so that increasingly one "holds loosely" all loves, with open hands and heart. To hold loosely is to let go of fearful clutching and control and to set free that which is loved.[11] This kind of liberating love grows slowly, gradually, and is not possible aside from the work of the night, for we are burdened with many attachments, addictions, and idolatry. We all struggle with "disordered affections," to use the language of Ignatius of Loyola.[12]

9. May, *The Dark Night of the Soul*, 8.

10. For a thorough discussion of the value of John's theology for those in recovery from addictions, see Nemeck and Coombs, *O Blessed Night*.

11. Sting captures the spirituality of this kind of liberating love, and the perennial problem of clutching and controlling those we love, in his song "If You Love Somebody, Set Them Free," *The Very Best of Sting and the Police*, A&M, 2002.

12. The Ignatian spiritual exercises are a systematic method of prayer and self-examination to help identify disordered affections and progress in the spiritual life. See Ignatius of Loyola, *Spiritual Exercises and Selected Works*, Classics of Western Spirituality, ed. George E. Ganss (Mahwah, NJ: Paulist, 1991), 113–214.

Questions for Reflection

1. In the tradition of John of the Cross and others, a dark night of the soul is initiated by God in order to liberate us and heal us of attachments so that we have greater capacity to receive and give love to God, to others, and to ourselves. Have you ever had to give up a habit or activity or some other attachment that was very difficult? Describe your experience. What did you learn about yourself in the process of struggle?

2. Many people want their church experience to be upbeat and to make them feel good. What would happen if people learned about the dark night of the soul in sermons and in small groups?

3. As you reflect upon this introductory information on the dark night of the soul, what are some questions that arise for you? *Why are we so resistant to God's correction? Is this perhaps a better way to address God's discipline roots?*

Jesus in the Wilderness

Jesus experienced the dark night of the soul twice: at the beginning of his ministry and at the end, on the cross. The story of his first dark night takes place in the desert wilds. This is the only account in the New Testament in which Jesus fasted. His emptiness was a physical manifestation of the spiritual anguish that is part of the dark night of the soul. According to the Gospel of Mark, after his baptism Jesus was driven immediately into the wilderness by the Holy Spirit. Matthew and Luke say the Holy Spirit led Jesus out to be tempted. What is most important for us to notice is that it was not Satan, nor was it failure on the part of

Jesus, but the Holy Spirit who initiated the wilderness experience. This dark night of the soul was part of Jesus's preparation for ministry. It was necessary.

Let's imagine ourselves in this story, perhaps as some of John the Baptist's disciples. We are there by the Jordan River where John, the cousin of Jesus, shouts to the teeming crowd. His looks are enough to stop conversation. As a Nazarite[13] Rabbi John has never cut his hair or beard. His rigid diet and life outdoors have hardened his body to sinew and bone. Our rabbi wears a rough garment made of camel hair and a leather belt. As we scan the crowd, we are amazed to see who is there: a strange collection of religious leaders, tax collectors, Roman soldiers, and workaday folk. We love John fiercely. And because of what he preaches, we fear for him:

> "You brood of vipers! Who warned you to flee from the wrath to come? Bear fruits worthy of repentance. Do not begin to say to yourselves, 'We have Abraham as our ancestor'; for I tell you, God is able from these stones to raise up children to Abraham. Even now the ax is lying at the root of the trees; every tree therefore that does not bear good fruit is cut down and thrown into the fire."

> And the crowds asked him, "What then should we do?" In reply he said to them, "Whoever has two coats must share with anyone who has none; and whoever has food must do likewise." Even tax collectors came to be bap-

---

13. The angel that appeared to Zachariah and announced that he and Elizabeth would have a child in their advanced age told Zachariah that the child, John, should never drink wine or strong drink and that he would be a prophet. This set of instructions was part of the Nazarite vow, an ancient custom in which men and women dedicated themselves, either for a limited time or for life, to prophetic witness. In addition to refraining from alcohol Nazarites did not cut their hair or shave, and in other ways practiced asceticism. See Numbers 6:1-8.

tized, and they asked him, "Teacher, what should we do?" He said to them, "Collect no more than the amount prescribed for you." Soldiers also asked him, "And we, what should we do?" He said to them, "Do not extort money from anyone by threats or false accusation, and be satisfied with your wages." (Luke 3:7b-14)

Suddenly Jesus steps out from the crowd, motioning that he wants to be baptized. Rabbi John resists, confused by the request. He doesn't know anyone more holy than Jesus, and we don't know anyone more holy than John. We hear John say to Jesus, "I need to be baptized by you, and do you come to me?" (Matthew 3:14b). The rabbi has been telling us for a while that someone more powerful than himself was coming who would baptize us "with the Holy Spirit and fire" (Matthew 3:11). Could he have meant his cousin, Jesus? Isn't Jesus the carpenter's son? What does he mean "with the Holy Spirit and fire"? We watch intensely, full of questions.

Jesus steps into the river. The look on his face tells us he will not be denied. Though Rabbi John does not fully understand why he must baptize Jesus, he agrees to do it. As Jesus emerges from the water, the heavens open. Incredibly, we see the divine radiance in the appearance of a dove descending upon him. God speaks from heaven: "This is my Son, the Beloved, with whom I am well pleased" (Matthew 3:16-17).

Whatever happens next, we know we have witnessed something too deep for words. We have seen and heard the God of Abraham, Isaac, and Jacob. Surely Jesus is the one we have awaited, the Messiah who will bring our salvation.

Immediately, the Holy Spirit drove Jesus into the wilderness, where he had to fast for forty days and nights—a phrase that in Jesus's day meant "a very long time." It was there in the wilderness after many days when Jesus was famished that Satan came to tempt him. When Jesus was at his weakest point, Satan came. Each of the three temptations had to do with his identity and call and with what kind of God, God is. Maddeningly, the temptations were cloaked in Scripture and memories of his baptism. The clarity he had at his baptism, the affirmation of his call, and his identity as God's beloved Son receded into the backdrop of the harsh desert with the tempter's insinuating voice. Jesus had to learn to remain faithful to his call and to the character of God despite his emotions, his bodily needs, and his loneliness. He had to recognize and reject interpretations of Scripture that harm instead of help. Each time he refuted Satan, each time he chose the path of faithfulness to God and his own identity as God's beloved Son, it was an act of holy celebration. Jesus made each choice based upon the goodness of God and the promises of God. Mark concludes the harrowing story with, "He was with the wild beasts; and the angels waited on him" (Mark 1:13).

Jesus was not driven into the wilderness because he was being punished or because he failed or because of any other wrongdoing on his part. Rather, he entered the wilderness in order to learn discernment. The wilds became for him a kind of Outward Bound[14] for the soul.

A Spirit-initiated dark night of the soul can have that effect on us. Spirit-ordained journeys through the wilderness are part of

14. Outward Bound is an experiential wilderness skills training program that nurtures courage, compassion, and confidence in participants. Lessons learned in Outward Bound apply to all of life. https://www.outwardbound.org/.

the faith journey for serious followers of Jesus. Jesus is our exemplar for traversing the wilds. But Jesus is more than that. Through the indwelling Holy Spirit, he is truly in us and with us because we—followers of Jesus—are the body of Christ in this world. We are never truly alone. The wilderness narrative now becomes our field guide anytime we find ourselves in the wilds, facing the tempter's voice.

Questions for Reflection

1. Some people resist thinking of God in any way except as perpetually gentle and "nice." Others think of God as a wrathful, jealous, punishing Father who is to be feared at all times. How does the story of Jesus's temptation in the wilderness correct those distorted images of God?

2. How does the story of Jesus in the wilderness subvert versions of discipleship in which following Jesus is reduced to attending worship, giving money to the church, and "being a good person"?

3. If this story from Jesus's life resonates with your own experience because you, too, have been led into a wilderness of testing, who or what were the wild beasts that were with you? Who or what were the angels that tended you?

Another Kind of Wilderness

In his 1989 classic work on Christian leadership *In the Name of Jesus*, Henri Nouwen argues that ministers in the twenty-first century would need to dwell in this wilderness narrative, for the same temptations that befell Jesus would haunt leaders in the new era of postmodernity. Framing the temptations for late twentieth century readers, Nouwen describes them as temptations to be relevant, popular, and powerful. Nouwen drew from his own experience as a priest and professor in order to name the universal challenges of spiritual leadership. More than that, Nouwen wrote this book after having left academia and a high-profile public speaking schedule in order to return to a deep, spiritual centeredness. He describes his own brokenness in this way: "I was living in a very dark place and the term 'burnout' was a convenient psychological translation for spiritual death."[15] His powerful insights about leadership for the future emerged as he found healing at L'Arche.

What ministers will need in order to be faithful to God and themselves, he argues, will likely seem counterintuitive. They will have to move from seeking relevance in ministry to seeking God in prayer, from seeking popularity to taking up a communal form of leadership with shared power, and from power in leadership to the humility of being led. These three transformations can only happen in the wilderness. These temptations and movements to authentic spiritual leadership all have to do with identity.

For Nouwen to regain authenticity himself, at the urging of friends he moved from the prestigious public life he had been living to L'Arche, a community of profoundly disabled people and their companions. Because of their intellectual disabilities, they were not able to be impressed with Nouwen's words, his having taught at Notre Dame, Yale, and Harvard, or anything else he had achieved. "I was suddenly faced with my naked self, open for

---

15. Henri J. M. Nouwen, *In the Name of Jesus: Reflections on Christian Leadership* (New York: Crossroad, 1989), Kindle edition, location 157.

affirmations and rejections, hugs and punches, smiles and tears, all dependent simply on how I was perceived at the moment."[16]

Coming face-to-face with his "naked self" was both disorienting and liberating for Nouwen, and that is the case for each of us. During his wilderness journey brought about by burnout, Nouwen found life in celebrating the Eucharist with his community at L'Arche. (We will explore the practice of celebration in the sacraments later in this book.)

We don't have to teach at Notre Dame or write books that millions of people read or live in a community of disabled people in order to encounter the kind of temptations Nouwen describes. We only have to be human and live in a broken world. One of the difficulties in facing these temptations is that they are always masked in normal human need for sustenance, affirmation, and a life of meaning.

Questions for Reflection

1. In this section we reflected on how burnout led Henri Nouwen to a pivotal life change with his move to the L'Arche community. Have you ever experienced burnout, which Nouwen also named as "spiritual death"? If so, what were the circumstances? How did you process what was happening? Were there people or resources that helped you make choices as you moved forward?

2. In his book *In the Name of Jesus*, Nouwen reinterpreted the three temptations of Jesus in the wilderness for Christian leaders in the new millennium. How would you interpret the three temptations in your own life?

16. Nouwen, *In the Name of Jesus*, location 183.

3. While Nouwen slowly healed in the L'Arche community, he served as priest there, regularly celebrating Holy Communion with the residents and their guests. Sharing in Communion became one of the primary ways he practiced celebration even in the midst of burnout. What are some ways you have practiced celebration during your own seasons of exhaustion and uncertainty about your spiritual life? — *God has always gotten me there & I trust him to keep doing it!*

4. Some of us go through the kind of "spiritual death" Nouwen described and are not able to find ways to celebrate at that time. We are simply too exhausted or filled with grief. If you ever had that experience, what do you wish you could have done in celebration as you look back?

5. It is a common human response to want to blame others when we experience burnout or some other dark night situation that results from our own choices. Fixing blame on others can actually keep us stuck in the wilderness instead of moving toward a new day. What might it look like to take appropriate responsibility for our own choices in this kind of situation, while yet exercising grace and compassion toward ourselves? In terms of practical actions, what might be helpful? What kind of support from friends, pastors, or others could help? Are there liturgical or sacramental actions that could help?

Can We Drink the Cup?

In the last book he wrote before his death in 1996, *Can You Drink the Cup?*, Nouwen focused on the Communion cup as a metaphor through which to understand all the events that make up the story of our lives.[17] With Nouwen, I believe the central questions for living our faith authentically are these: Can we actually embrace our life as it is, with all the sorrow and joy that commingle, with all our brilliant and mundane moments, our human frailty and exquisite beauty? Can we celebrate the fact that God is with us in all of it, holding us close, telling us that we, too, are God's beloved and in us God is well-pleased? Can we find our identity in being loved just as Jesus did at his baptism, prior to his temptation in the wilderness? And can we trust that through thick and thin God's love will sustain us even in our dark nights of the soul?

These questions came home to me in a powerful new way as I prepared to graduate with a PhD in systematic theology. I was serving as a pastor at the time, and one of my relatives asked if I would officiate at her wedding. Pleased to be asked, I quickly agreed. My siblings and mother and some extended family gathered for the occasion on the west coast, which was no small feat.[18] For various reasons big family reunions have been quite rare for us, even though we love each other very much and do stay in touch. The morning of the day before the wedding, we were to gather for an early breakfast in a conference room at the hotel where we were staying.

At the appointed hour I walked into the room and was astounded to see everyone else there, grinning from ear to ear. My sister Jeanine walked toward me carrying a graduation cap and gown. They were made of paper but looked realistic. "Hi, Sis," she laughed. "We wanted to surprise you with a graduation party, and this was the only time slot we could find!" I looked around the

---

17. Henri J. M. Nouwen, *Can You Drink the Cup?* (Notre Dame, IN: Ave Maria Press, 1996).

18. My father had died a few years prior to this event. Like my mother, he came to faith late in life. I like to think that had he been able he would have been there with us. My mother had come to love Jesus a few years before this graduation party.

table at my family, speechless. Nothing like this had ever happened to me. My siblings and I all left home when we were still children because of the violence and chaos that marked our daily lives. I left when I was sixteen, still a junior in high school. We each found ways to get by as we finished growing up, staying with neighbors or wherever we could. It is a marvel that all five of us managed to get through high school, much less all of us making it to college. For a host of reasons related to our fragmented childhood, none of my siblings or parents attended any of the milestone events in my life, including graduation from high school, getting married, giving birth, my children's accomplishments and graduations, my graduation from college in my late thirties, and then graduation from seminary in my forties. Nor was I able to be present with them at such times.

And now here they were, holding a graduation party for me at a nice hotel at 8:00 in the morning. My mother's eyes glistened with tears of joy.[19] After we ate a hearty breakfast, Jeanine pulled out a copy of Henri Nouwen's *Can You Drink the Cup,* and began to read aloud. She had chosen an excerpt from it about the courage it takes to embrace one's own life with all its brokenness and promise. She concluded the reading with Nouwen's words: "Drinking our cup is a hopeful, courageous, and self-confident way of living. It is standing in the world with head erect, solidly rooted in the knowledge of who we are, facing the reality that surrounds us and responding to it from our hearts."[20]

19. A few weeks later she flew to my graduation ceremony where she sat in the front row, cheering and clapping wildly when I was hooded. Though she was eighty-three and suffering from multiple health challenges, she was determined to be there this time.

20. Nouwen, *Can You Drink the Cup?* Kindle edition, location 475–77.

"Our family has not had an easy time," Jeanine said. "We have all had our challenges. And yet look at us. Look at how we love each other despite all of that, and how we are here together at this table. God is with us at the table and is with Elaine in her calling. We are here to support you, Elaine, and let you know how proud of you we are. You have stood in the world with your head erect, solidly rooted in the knowledge of who you are, facing the reality that surrounds you, and doing so from your heart. We salute you." With that, she pulled out a beautiful Communion chalice and paten. "We are going to each write a blessing for Elaine," she instructed our family, "and put it in this cup. This is a Blessing Cup for Elaine."

In that moment, as tears streamed down our faces, all the joy and sorrow of our family's journey merged with the joy and sorrow of Jesus. It was a moment of profound healing for all of us. One by one my family members read their little notes of blessing, folded the notes, and put them in the cup. When Jeanine handed me the cup overflowing with blessings, I was unable to speak or do anything but cry. All these years later I still cannot recall this event without tears.

The cup of life—your life and my life—is a cup of celebration not because we have an easy life, not because we are problem free, but because God loves us. We celebrate because God is with us and for us. God is absolutely committed to making all things new, and the wondrous thing is, we get to be part of that process for one another. That day my sister was the love of God made flesh, calling us to the table, bringing us to new depths of healing and reconciliation. In sharing a Blessing Cup, Jeanine boldly declared that deeper than all the pain we had experienced, we belonged to one another and to God. We were God's beloved children, in whom God was well-pleased.

Rachel's Story

Rachel was a dedicated, lifelong Christian and faithful church member.[21] She always attended worship and Sunday school and sang in the choir. As a local elementary school teacher, she knew many of the families living in her small town. Always a responsible person and a self-identified "rule follower," Rachel took seriously the strict morality she learned in her church. Among other things, Rachel learned that it was sinful to get divorced regardless of the reason. She was taught that anyone who gets divorced is under God's wrath and will go to hell, and that anyone who is divorced and remarries commits adultery and will go to hell.

When she was twenty-five, Rachel married a charming man who seemed to adore her and often said that he wanted to take care of her. Within months of their wedding, though, he began to abuse her. At first it was verbal, then sexual, then the violence escalated with punches, kicks, and hair pulled out. Rachel never knew what would set him off. Her life became a nightmare as she lived through the cycle of domestic violence over and over and was increasingly isolated from her family and friends.[22] She had to miss school sometimes because of the physical and emotional pain he inflicted.

21. Here and elsewhere I have changed names and identifying details of stories in order to protect the privacy of individuals.

22. For more information about the Cycle of Domestic Violence see Jennifer Focht, "The Cycle of Domestic Violence," National Center for Health Research, 2019, http://www.center4research.org/cycle-domestic-violence/.

When Rachel finally approached her pastor and told him about the violence he said, "You, young lady, are the problem. You need to submit to your husband. He is the head of the home, and if you will take better care of him, he will come around. It's your job to model a meek and Christlike spirit so that he will hunger for God and take better care of you. Have you been rebellious toward him? Have you been proud? That's usually what causes these problems." Rachel left the pastor's office filled with shame and confusion. The pastor seemed to say the abuse was her fault, and while part of her believed that message because it came from the pastor, a quiet voice within her said it was not true. In her heart she knew she did not deserve to be battered regardless of how she might disappoint her husband.

One day Rachel was at the kitchen sink washing dishes when her husband abruptly demanded that she get rid of their puppy. "I never said you could get it!" he shouted, his face red and threatening. "I'm sick and tired of having to cater to you and what you want. What about what I want?" Before she could respond, he threw a chair at her, knocking her to the floor. Dazed and bleeding, Rachel pretended to be unconscious so he would leave her alone. After shouting profanities at her, he stormed out of the house and drove away. Rachel gathered a few clothes, her purse, and the puppy. She looked at her well-worn Bible, thought of the pastor's accusing words, and left it sitting on the table.

That night at the women's shelter, Rachel met a woman who told her that it wasn't God's will for her to suffer abuse. It was the first time Rachel heard a Christian speak in this way. She was worried that the woman was a "liberal" but grateful for the woman's kindness. Over time, with therapy, assistance, many setbacks, and hard work, Rachel found strength to divorce the man whose abuse had destroyed their marriage. In the process she had to go through a wilderness journey in which she, like Henri Nouwen, had to encounter her "naked self." She eventually encountered God in ways she never knew were possible.

Rachel's healing journey led her into what many spiritual writers refer to as "liminal space," or the threshold between what is known and familiar to a new and initially disorienting reality. Rachel's horizon shifted massively as she wrestled toward a much bigger vision of God and more loving and self-respecting posture toward herself. The temptations in the wilderness for Rachel had to do with her identity as a Christian; what kind of God, God is; and with the healing process that required establishing boundaries for herself. At first she felt as if she had been swallowed up in spiritual darkness because she was sure she had committed an unforgivable sin in leaving her violent partner. Gradually, with the help of a small recovery group and a gifted facilitator, she came to see that God gave her strength to leave the abuse. Over time Rachel questioned her faith and considered leaving Christianity altogether because of the harm perpetuated by her former pastor and church. But with a spiritual director, Rachel was able to find a deep relationship with God that was life-giving for herself and others. Today Rachel is a wise and compassionate Christian whose journey has enabled her to be a strong advocate for others who suffer.

In his best-selling book *Falling Upward: A Spirituality for the Two Halves of Life*, Richard Rohr explores the pattern of a dark night followed by enlightenment that so many people experience around midlife.[23] In this pattern, inevitably the accepted view of

23. Richard Rohr, *Falling Upward: A Spirituality for the Two Halves of Life* (San Francisco: Jossey-Bass, 2011).

God, self, and the world that "worked" during the first half of life no longer fits with lived experience. Sometimes this awareness happens gradually, without a lot of drama. At other times something happens that blows one's worldview apart: a divorce, a death, a betrayal, coming out, or as in Rachel's case, awakening to how we have unwittingly participated in our own oppression because of dysfunctional beliefs. Whether it happens suddenly or slowly, our lived experience no longer jibes with what until that time we believed about God, ourselves, and the world. As the rug is pulled out from beneath our former worldview, we are driven into liminal space where we must struggle to make meaning in our strange, new world. At that point, Rohr says, "What looks like falling can largely be experienced as falling upward and onward, into a broader and deeper world, where the soul has found its fullness, is finally connected to the whole, and lives inside the Big Picture. It is not a loss but somehow a gain, not losing but actually winning."[24]

Questions for Reflection

1. Sometimes we experience a type of dark night because of the choices and actions of other people. This is true for survivors of trauma caused by war, childhood abuse and neglect, bullying, or intimate partner violence. It is also true for racial, ethnic, and sexual minorities and others who experience systemic marginalization and oppression by the dominant culture. In this situation the dark night can become a season leading to liberation, as in Rachel's case. Spend a few moments reflecting upon the people in your neighborhood and larger community. Who comes

24. Rohr, *Falling Upward*, 153.

to mind as individuals or groups who may be experiencing this kind of dark night? How might the church creatively and compassionately companion people like Rachel?

2. Sometimes in the church people feel shamed and silenced by leaders for expressing doubts about God, faith, and the church when they are "falling upward." What might be some ways the church could help people celebrate God's presence during a dark night of doubt and uncertainty and the disorientation of "falling upward"?

Conclusion

Dark night of the soul, the wilderness, the desert, a cloud of unknowing, winter—these are all terms great Christian saints and mystics have used to describe seasons in which God seems to have disappeared or seems to have become silent. God's presence is no longer felt affectively as before, and previous theological positions no longer make sense in light of lived experience. There are three other signs of a dark night that characterize this kind of suffering. These are (1) dryness and fruitlessness in prayer, religious activity, and life; (2) a loss of desire for the old ways of being religious; and (3) a growing desire simply to be with God. These signs of a dark night are related to the person's relationship (or not) to a faith community. Often they are experienced with deep distress, confusion, and grief.

Because of my research, writing, and teaching about the emergence of new forms of Christian community, I frequently hear from people who are immersed in these three phenomena. I commonly hear statements like these:

1. I no longer believe in the kind of hell I learned about in Sunday school as a kid. It doesn't make sense to me anymore because I can't imagine God loving us less than I love my kids. I can't imagine how God could torture people forever and never give them a way out. What kind of God would do that? Does it mean that I am no longer a Christian because I can't believe in that kind of hell? I just wish I could be with people who believe in the God of love instead of a God of hate.

2. I used to think that LGBTQ people were sinful and wrong because they chose a sinful lifestyle and could not be Christians. I thought they needed to be repro- grammed or something. Then I found out my son is one of "them." He's gay, says he knew it from as far back as he can remember, and I don't know anyone who is more compassionate and Jesus-like than my son. What amazes me is that he is still a Christian despite me and so many other ignorant people. Now I'm questioning everything I was taught about the Christian faith and the Bible. I'm not sure I can stay in the church. I haven't been able to read the Bible for at least two years. I don't know what to believe now. I just know I'm going to support my son.

3. I used to love everything about the church: singing in the choir, listening to the sermon, teaching in vacation Bible school, all of it. When the doors were open, I was there. Now I find it all feels empty. I can barely make myself go to church anymore. I skip church a lot because it feels so meaningless, and I can't even tell you how this all started. I still believe in God. I still love Jesus. I just wish it could be simpler and that we could go deeper, without all the programs and committees and night after night of exhausting activities.

4. I was raised in a very prestigious church where everything is done with excellence. My home church is proud of its liturgy, the professional choir, the beauty of its buildings. Our pastors all have doctoral degrees. They can hold their own with anyone. I used to find all those things meaningful, but now all I can think about is what does this have to do with the homeless guys sitting out on the church step through the week? I think I'm going to have to leave the church I grew up in because it seems dead to me now. But I don't know where to go or what to do. I can't get those homeless guys out of my mind.

5. I came to faith in a Pentecostal church in my teens. They really welcomed me, and I loved the praise band and the way the pastor's sermons were so practical. But for some reason all of that exhausts me now. I long for something more quiet and dignified. Something simple. I visited a Quaker meeting once and liked it because no one talked. It was mostly a bunch of people just sitting there. To be honest I feel closer to God in my deer stand than I do in church anymore because it's so quiet. Do you think I'm a heretic because of this? I just don't know what to do.

Perhaps one or more of these questions resonates with you or with someone you love. If so, I pray that this book will help you to know that God is very near when we are in a dark night, when we are in the wilderness. God is always much bigger than we think, more merciful, more loving, and more intent upon our well-being than we know. The practice of Christian celebration during your season in the dark night does not mean you have to deny your experience or pretend to feel differently than you do. It means honestly naming what you are feeling and thinking to God and, if possible, to a trusted spiritual friend or spiritual director who can companion you at this time. To pray in this way is an act of celebration, trusting that God is leading you through the wilderness just as God did with Jesus. And as the Holy Spirit broods over the chaos at the beginning of Creation (Genesis 1:2), bringing forth beautiful new life, the Holy Spirit broods over us in the dark night like a mother bird protecting her young in the nest.

God's love created you. God's love holds you. God's love will never let you go.

Chapter Two

Memory

I stood at the edge of Bruce's grave, marveling that in light of his family history, all his children had come together to mourn him and put him to rest.[1] We were in a national cemetery for veterans with row upon row of white crosses. Maria, Bruce's wife, had told me some years back that when he returned from Viet Nam, he was not the same man she had married. Tormented with what we now call post-traumatic stress disorder, Bruce developed multiple addictions in an effort to quell the demons within. Their life together was often hellish, especially when the children were growing up. Maria came close to leaving him many times but never did. Her eyes always looked sad, even when she laughed.

Bruce and Maria's children grew up in terror of their father because of his unpredictable rage. Some of them developed addictions of their own because of the trauma they carried from those years. Even his adult children who were people of faith found it

---

1. Here as elsewhere I have changed names and identifying details to protect the privacy of persons in the story.

nearly impossible to forgive Bruce for the pain he had inflicted upon their family.

It is not easy to help people prepare for a funeral in situations of this kind. When an aging parent dies with "unfinished business" with family, so many tensions, memories, unmet expectations, and resentments can surface, reigniting pain that everyone thought they had outgrown. In alcoholic families in particular, children often grow up following an unspoken script in which each child is assigned a persona: the star, the slacker, the hero, the con artist, the smart one, the bimbo, the good one, the dumb one. Often one child is targeted as a scapegoat. Regardless of how much healing adult children of alcoholics experience, at times like this it is easy to slip back into those roles, to everyone's detriment. I remembered all of this and saw signs of it surfacing as I worked with the family. Nonetheless, I felt confident that we had made a good plan together and were ready for a meaningful service in which we would celebrate Bruce's life. Now we stood in the chilly breeze, a small cluster of Maria and her boys with their wives and children.

Holding a smooth stone about the size of an egg, I invited the family members to come forward so that we could "raise an Ebenezer," or create a pile of stones to remember and celebrate stories of how God had been with Bruce throughout his life, helping him even when Bruce did not know it. During our planning I acknowledged the pain of the family. I then offered a theology of grace, saying that God knew Bruce's entire story and had mercy on Bruce. God understood the ways Bruce was traumatized during the war. Within this vision of mercy and grace, I said, God loved Bruce despite his many failures. It is very difficult to try to parse the difference between being harmed, behaving dysfunctionally as a coping mechanism after the harm, having one's spirituality distorted by the harm, and willfully passing sin on to others, I explained. Only God knows everything about us. Because of that I trusted that God loved Bruce and helped him and had mercy on him. The family seemed to accept this concept of grace, although one of Bruce's sons asked about damnation.

We finally came to agreement that the Ebenezer ritual would help everyone say goodbye to Bruce honorably. It would be a simple way to provide a collective eulogy from family members that was authentic and gracious despite the pain of their story. The dozen or so family members formed a semicircle around me, each carrying a stone he or she had carefully chosen for this purpose. A small table next to the grave had been prepared for the ritual. Suddenly Maria rushed forward. "No, no, NO!" she shouted, clutching my arm and causing me to drop my stone, which promptly bounced into the hole and hit the coffin. "Don't let them throw rocks at him. I admit, he was a terrible father. I always knew it. But I can't let them do this!"

Despite all my careful planning and theological explanations with the family about the meaning of the stones, Maria was clueless. Because of stress, she tuned out all my fancy theology words as we planned the funeral. Historically, she had defended Bruce when the boys lashed out to her about their dad. She always had an excuse for him. Like many partners of alcoholics, she was enmeshed with him, codependent with his addiction. So it was at his graveside that she leapt to his defense once again to protect him from what she thought would be an attack.

"Preacher!" yelled one of the sons, face red, fists balled. "Good God, when will this end?"

"Here we go," said another in disgust.

It took some doing to get everyone to settle down and finish the service. But we did. Afterward, as we ate potato salad, Maria leaned toward me looking sheepish. In a conspiratorial whisper she said, "Bruce would have hated that funeral. He didn't want one. But you know what? I don't care. But don't you dare tell them kids."

Questions for Reflection

1. When you read the story of Bruce, Maria, and their family, did anything about it resonate with your personal experience?

2. Have you ever experienced a funeral that was joyous even in the midst of loved ones' grief? If so, describe what happened and why it felt joyful.

3. Some people think that individuals like Bruce are beyond God's reach and cannot be in God's presence unless they repent of their sin and undergo a significant personality change. Yet in this story the pastor believed and told the family that God was with Bruce throughout his life, even when Bruce did not know it. Bruce was part of God's story. Reflect on this theology of grace and mercy.

4. *Gran Torino* is a movie with a number of themes similar to Bruce's story.[2] Consider watching the movie with others, and discuss the characters' struggles to reconcile religious beliefs with the complexity of the main character's life.

2. *Gran Torino*, directed by Clint Eastwood, produced by Double Nickel Entertainment, 2008, 120 min.

Ebenezer

Perhaps you remember the line from the second stanza of the famous hymn "Come, Thou Fount of Every Blessing," which says, "Here I raise mine Ebenezer, hither by thy help I'm come."[3] The Hebrew word *Ebenezer* means "stone of help." To raise an Ebenezer is to erect a stone or pile of stones to commemorate and celebrate God's victory over enemies. The biblical story upon which this hymn is based is found in 1 Samuel 7.

The prophet Samuel was the last judge over Israel when he anointed Saul to become its first king. A judge in that period of ancient Israel's history was a combined civic, military, and religious leader. Stories of the judges leading up to Samuel are repeating narratives of generational dysfunction in which God's people start out well enough, honoring and worshiping God in ways that are countercultural and that bear witness to the love of God. They start out living according to the patterns given to them by Moses. But inevitably they begin to compromise their commitments to God, marry people with appalling religious practices including child sacrifice, and before you know it everyone is doing whatever they please in a culture riddled with violence.

The repeating line throughout the book of Judges is, "In those days there was no king in Israel; all the people did what was right in their own eyes" (21:25). Because of social fragmentation caused by violence and lawlessness, they became vulnerable to marauding neighbors who then overpowered and subjugated them. When God's people were utterly defeated, living in bondage, they repented

3. Robert Robinson, lyrics, 1758, "Come, Thou Fount of Every Blessing," *The United Methodist Hymnal* (Nashville: The United Methodist Publishing House, 1989), no. 400.

of what they had done and cried out to God, who forgave them and sent a leader—a judge—to help them find peace again. When that happened, they celebrated. These "R-rated" stories of judges rival anything Hollywood has to offer. Judges is not a children's book!

Samuel came on the scene at the end of the judge narrative cycles and appears in 1 Samuel. In this story he rallies Israel once again, calling them to repentance for the ways they have sinned against God. As they successfully defeat the Philistines, their attackers, they celebrate God's victory by raising an Ebenezer.

This story has something important in common with narratives like that of Bruce and Maria's family, especially as we consider the practice of celebration. Both the Judges narrative cycles and families like Bruce's suffer from what the Bible describes as "generational iniquity" (Exodus 34:7, Ezekiel 18:20). That is to say, the consequences of destructive behavior, poor choices, and the like play out for generations after the original actors. Genograms (family trees that focus on relationships and patterns of behavior that are generational) are visual representations of this tendency.[4]

While there seems to be a genetic predisposition toward addiction in some people, there is also an environmental factor. Children who grow up in families with addictions are more likely to become addicted themselves. The same is true for children growing up with experiences of neglect, abuse, and other adverse family experiences.

In the late 1990s Kaiser Permanente launched a major research project to try to determine how adverse childhood experiences can affect children's trajectories in adulthood.[5] The result of

4. For an introduction to genograms and several helpful links for further study, see https://www.genopro.com/genogram/.
5. Adverse Childhood Experiences (ACEs), https://www.cdc.gov/violenceprevention/childabuseandneglect/acestudy/index.html.

the study was staggering, partly because of the magnitude of its findings and partly because it took many more years before mental health professionals and educators took seriously the impact of such experiences on children.[6]

According to the study, there are ten types of experiences that dramatically affect children's future struggles as adults. The ten include physical, emotional, or sexual abuse; physical or emotional neglect; mental illness; seeing the mother treated violently; divorce; an incarcerated relative; and substance abuse.[7] If people experience at least four out of the ten adverse childhood experiences, the likelihood of future trauma increases exponentially. The higher the score, the more likely the child will experience debilitating dysfunction and suffering in adult life.

The church can support the recovery and healing of individuals and families with a history of adverse childhood experiences in numerous ways: good pastoral care, recovery groups, sermons that connect with the experiences people have, and educational programs that prevent and heal sexual abuse and domestic violence. Pastors can offer compassionate care during life's crises and transitions, including illness and death. But the church and pastors can also learn much from people in the recovery communities. The spirituality of twelve-step programs including Alcoholics Anonymous forms genuine community that helps people to heal and remain sober. I have heard many recovering alcoholics say that AA is their church because there they find the authenticity, humility, and healthy community they need, as well as coming to depend upon God as their "higher power."

---

6. For more about the slowness of the helping professions to act upon the ACEs study, see Bessel van der Kolk, *The Body Keeps the Score: Brain, Mind, and Body in the Healing of Trauma* (New York: Penguin, 2014), 87, 146–50, 158, 349, 352–53.

7. Van der Kolk, *The Body Keeps the Score.*

Moreover, I have rarely seen more robust celebrations than when a friend says, with joyful amazement, "Today marks ten years of sobriety!" In the recovery community, no one wants or tries to forget their own story. Instead, they learn to remember, accept, honor, and learn from their story. Twelve-step spirituality helps them to do that. Through practices of celebrating their milestones of sobriety, or freedom from violence, or deliverance from some other kind of bondage, people in recovery say "no" to the death-dealing choices of the past, including generational iniquity, and "yes" to life for the future.

Questions for Reflection

1. Why is it important for persons in recovery to remember their stories intentionally? Why not "leave the past in the past"? Is it possible to leave the past behind and yet remember our whole story of deliverance? If so, how might we do this?

2. In ancient Hebrew culture, raising an Ebenezer was a tangible way to celebrate God's victory over their enemies. Since antiquity many cultures around the world have used stacked stones or standing stones in religious rituals. Have you ever seen or created a cairn or some other form of stacked stone as a way to commemorate a spiritually important moment? If so, how did this experience impact you emotionally, spiritually, or relationally?

3. Either by yourself or with a small group of trusted friends, create an Ebenezer in which you celebrate and share stories of how God has helped you.

When Memory Is Lost

In the profound book *In Memory's Kitchen*, Cara de Silva tells the story of starving Jewish women who were interred in Terezín, a concentration camp in Czechoslovakia during World War II. The camp was unique in that it was in a ghetto in the city and was used for propaganda to falsely claim that incarcerated persons were treated well. In an act of celebratory memory in the face of unspeakable evil, the women of Terezin wrote recipes for their favorite foods, filling the pages with dishes they remembered cooking, in the hope that their daughters and granddaughters would survive and keep the stories of their families alive.[8] The book includes recipes along with explanatory notes from the editors. Most of the women of Terezin were sent on to Auschwitz, where they perished. Yet through their recipes and notes, their stories do live on.

Jewish history is riddled with stories of persecution, displacement, and exile, both in the Bible and after the Bible was written. The book of Exodus, the story of the Israelites escaping slavery in Egypt, is the pivotal narrative of the entire Hebrew Bible. It begins with the first holocaust in Jewish history. Pharaoh ordered Hebrew midwives to kill every baby boy who was born to Hebrew women because there were "too many Hebrews," which he saw as a threat since they were slaves. He feared an uprising.

The Israelites originally migrated to Egypt when the Hebrew Joseph was a high-ranking official. Because of his respect for and trust in Joseph, Pharaoh welcomed Joseph's people during a

---

8. Cara de Silva, with preface by Michael Berenbaum, translated by Bianca Steiner Brown, *In Memory's Kitchen: A Legacy from the Women of Terezin* (Lanham, MD: Jason Aronson, 2006).

famine.[9] But after many years, the last pharaoh who remembered Joseph's story died. A xenophobic new pharaoh rose who did not know the history and began to rule over the Hebrew "outsiders" without mercy. Thus, they were enslaved. One of the themes that makes this story so compelling is the collective loss and retrieval of memory—memories of their own history and identity as a people, which are inseparable from memories of God.

According to Exodus 12:40-41, the Hebrew people were slaves in Egypt for four hundred thirty years.[10] While there was some resistance among the Hebrews, notably Shiphrah and Puah, the midwives who broke the law to save the infant Moses's life, the story presents a people thoroughly broken by captivity (Exodus 1:15-22). Though the people cried out to God because of their suffering, it seems they were not clear about God's identity. This is apparent from Moses's response when God called him to lead the deliverance of the Israelites from slavery:

> But Moses said to God, "If I come to the Israelites and say to them, 'The God of your ancestors has sent me to you,' and they ask me, 'What is his name?' what shall I say to them?" God said to Moses, "I AM WHO I AM." He said further, "Thus you shall say to the Israelites, 'I AM has sent me to you.'" God also said to Moses, "Thus you shall say to the Israelites, 'The LORD, the God of your ancestors, the God of Abraham, the God of Isaac, and the God of Jacob, has sent me to you':
>
> > This is my name forever,
> > and this my title for all generations." (Exodus 3:13-15)

9. Genesis 37–50 chronicles the inspiring story of Joseph, his brothers, their violence toward him, his persecution as a slave, and his subsequent rise to power in Egypt, where he eventually saves his people's lives.

10. Commentators disagree about the exact length of time that elapsed between Abraham and Moses. Nonetheless God told Abraham that his descendants would be enslaved for four hundred years (Genesis 15:13), and Exodus 12:40-41 correlates with that prediction so most traditional streams of biblical interpretation accept the approximately four-hundred-year time period.

In calling Moses's (and Israel's) attention to Abraham, Isaac, and Jacob, God retrieved for them the stories of their ancestral faith. With that connection came a renewal of Abraham and Sarah's call to become a blessing to the whole world (Genesis 12:1-3). Moreover, God's name is "I AM," a verb of continuous being. God had not forgotten the Hebrews, and the promises God made to Abraham and Sarah were still true. God was present and would act. This encounter between Moses and God launched the liberation movement. With the Exodus came a new story for God's people, one that would indeed be a blessing to the whole world. The resurrection of their lost story as God's people was an essential foundation for the Israelites to move from captivity to freedom, from despair to a good future.

Questions for Reflection

1. In the story of the Exodus, we learn that a new pharaoh came to power who did not know the story of Joseph, which led him to fear and enslave the Israelites. As you look at contemporary society, where do you see parallels with the loss of story and the oppression of people?

2. In order for the Israelites to move toward freedom, they needed to reconnect with their own original identity as a people and with God, who called forth the Israelite people. How does identity impact our capacity for celebration today?

3. What did Moses and the Israelite people have to give up in order to reclaim their true identity and story? How did their process of "giving up" free them to celebrate?

Chapter Two

A New Story

The loss and retrieval of Israel's story is a major theme throughout the Old Testament and is deeply tied to their capacity for celebration. When God's people forgot who they were, they forgot who God is and forgot their call to be a blessing to the world. Inevitably, this trajectory led them into bondage. Often their captivity was literal, as they were overrun by enemies, exiled, or killed, and their homes and land were taken away. At such times the temptation to despair was overwhelming.

Psalm 137 expresses the sharp grief of exiled Hebrews forced to listen to the taunts of their Babylonian captors:[11]

> By the rivers of Babylon—
>> there we sat down and there we wept
>> when we remembered Zion.
> On the willows there
>> we hung up our harps.
> For there our captors
>> asked us for songs,
> and our tormentors asked for mirth, saying,
>> "Sing us one of the songs of Zion!"
>
> How could we sing the LORD's song
>> in a foreign land?
> If I forget you, O Jerusalem,
>> let my right hand wither!
> Let my tongue cling to the roof of my mouth,
>> if I do not remember you,
> if I do not set Jerusalem
>> above my highest joy. (verses 1-6)

---

11. The Babylonian exile began on March 16, 597 BCE, with people from Judah being taken captive to Babylon. The exile ended in 538 BCE when Cyrus the Great allowed the people to return to their homeland.

When God delivered them from Babylon and they returned to Zion, their joy overflowed with some of the most beautiful language in the Psalms:

> When the LORD restored the fortunes of Zion,
> we were like those who dream.
> Then our mouth was filled with laughter,
> and our tongue with shouts of joy;
> then it was said among the nations,
> "The LORD has done great things for them."
> The LORD has done great things for us,
> and we rejoiced.
> Restore our fortunes, O LORD,
> like the watercourses in the Negeb.
> May those who sow in tears
> reap with shouts of joy.
> Those who go out weeping,
> bearing the seed for sowing,
> shall come home with shouts of joy,
> carrying their sheaves. (Psalm 126)

Sometimes the more insidious captivity, a type that is harder to liberate and heal after physical deliverance, is the colonization of God's people's imagination through syncretism, or the blend of their religion with elements of other religious cultures that seriously damage their faith. Often in the history of Israel this was part of cultural and political captivity. But sometimes syncretism was the result of Israel longing to be like everyone else in the surrounding cultures. For example, they combined Judaism with Canaanite fertility cults that included temple prostitution and human sacrifice. Syncretism was a particular snare in the time of the kings. Prophets such as Elijah and Elisha became God's way of calling Israel to return to true worship, to give up false gods

Key

41

and despicable practices and return to their true identity as people through whom the whole world was blessed. All of the major and minor prophets of the Old Testament carried out their difficult work in order to bring God's people back to God's original intent, which was to be a people who bless the world.

Questions for Reflection

1. Syncretism is the blend of our faith with incompatible religious practices and cultures. For ancient Israel, this meant combining Judaism with Canaanite fertility cults that included temple prostitution and human sacrifice. Syncretism damages our ability to remember the true God and the stories of God's true love for us. What are some of the forms syncretism takes today in our culture? How can we resist these forms of syncretism? What are some simple ways to become aware of how much syncretism affects our understanding of our Christian faith?

2. Just as Israel's imagination had been colonized by slavery, the church's imagination in the global west and north has been colonized by materialism, capitalism, and consumerism. How do these three cultural norms damage the church's sense of identity and its mission? How do these norms affect our images of God?

Celebrating God in the Neighborhood

With Jesus, God entered our human story in an unprecedented way. "The Word became flesh and blood, and moved into the neighborhood," as *The Message* puts it in John 1:14. Jesus's story reveals a face of God that astounds us even to this day. He certainly was not the type of Savior faithful Jews expected. Why would the almighty God, Creator of heaven and earth, choose to be born to an unwed mother from a persecuted religious minority in small, occupied region of Palestine? Why did shepherds, of all people, who were considered "unclean" by the rest of society, come to worship the newborn Christ? Why would God choose a life that included poverty, refugee status, a hometown with a bad reputation, and an adult life that would be cut short by a broken justice system, public torture, and murder at the city dump? Jesus was not a member of any kind of elite group, nor was he highly educated, nor was he a leader in the religious establishment. He worked with his hands. What does all of this tell us about God's priorities? And what does it tell us about ours?

John 1:18 says, "No one has ever seen God. It is God the only Son, who is close to the Father's heart, who has made him known." The apostle Paul tells us in Colossians 1:15 that Jesus is the image, or icon, of the invisible God. Everything about Jesus's birth, life, teaching, priorities, friends, enemies, suffering, death, and resurrection reveals God to us. Jesus shows us by his life what kind of God, God is. Jesus's life, even more than his words, becomes the interpretive key for the rest of the Bible for Christians. We find his life story in the Gospels.

And what we see in Jesus's life is a God who thoroughly lives into our neighborhoods. He understands our lives because he has been there. No aspect of human suffering, need, or temptation is foreign to him. He knows firsthand the joys of human life. Jesus reveals to us a God who knows us intimately and is in solidarity

with us in our human condition. This is why we can never celebrate his love too much.

Years ago, I visited a family to talk with the grandfather who was
leaning toward the Christian faith but had many doubts and objec-
tions. I love these friendships with people who do not yet know the
God who moved into our neighborhood. It is a joy to companion
people as they move toward genuine relationship with Jesus.

Several of the man's family were faithful Christians. We were
outdoors where his grandchildren were playing in the yard. He
confessed to me that he was worried about his two-year-old granddaughter because she was "too religious." Curious, I asked what he
meant. "She sings about Jesus all the time. Look at her," he ges-
tured toward the tiny girl who was digging in the dirt. "She's doing it now." I listened and sure enough, the words of "Jesus Loves
Me" floated up from where she was playing: "Yes, Jesus woves me.
The Bible tells me so."

"Why is this a problem?" I asked, truly puzzled.

"It's not natural," he said. "A kid that young shouldn't think
about religion. I think her parents are too religious. They might
even be fanatics. I don't know." His brow furrowed with concern.
I wondered what kind of life experiences had formed this man to
be suspicious of a young child's faith.

Eventually that grandfather came to faith and discovered for
himself the simplicity and purity of his granddaughter's love for
Jesus. Every time we sing to God from our hearts, we celebrate
the God who became flesh and blood and moved into the messy,
troubled, and ordinary neighborhoods of this world. Every act of
corporate and private worship, every prayer, every moment that
we intentionally choose a posture of love and trust toward Jesus,
we celebrate the God who became flesh and blood, who became
part of our story by moving into our neighborhood.

Questions for Reflection

1. Why would the almighty God, Creator of heaven and earth, choose to be born to an unwed mother from a persecuted religious minority in small, occupied region of Palestine? Why would God choose a life that included poverty, refugee status, a hometown with a bad reputation, and an adult life that would be cut short by a broken justice system, public torture, and murder at the city dump?

2. Because Jesus shows through his life and death compassion and solidarity for people who suffer injustice and bigotry, we can be sure that issues of injustice are important to God. What is the relationship between the spiritual practice of celebration and participating with God in addressing injustice in our neighborhoods?

3. In the story of the grandfather, he thought his granddaughter was "too religious." Is it possible to be "too religious"? What is the difference between being spiritually alive in a healthy way and being "too religious"? How might the spiritual practice of celebration protect people from unhealthy religiosity?

Remembering Our Story through the Sacraments[12]

Christians intentionally commit themselves to love, trust, follow, and identify with the Jesus of the Gospels through two embodied forms of prayer. In most historic Christian traditions,

---

12. Portions of this section first appeared in Elaine A. Heath, *Five Means of Grace: Experiencing God's Love the Wesleyan Way* (Nashville: Abingdon, 2018), 27–34. Used with permission.

these are called sacraments, which are "outward signs of inwardly received grace." Some traditions refer to these liturgical acts as "ordinances." Both of these—baptism and Holy Communion (also called the Lord's Supper and Eucharist)—are corporate practices of celebration that help Christians remember the story of Jesus within the long story arc of the whole Bible. Through baptism and Holy Communion, Christians intentionally place themselves within that story in order to give themselves to God's mission of making all things new.

Many Christians, including Methodists (my tribe), use some version of an ancient baptismal language in which we "renounce the forces of wickedness and reject the evil powers of this world." We accept our call to "resist evil, injustice, and oppression in whatever forms they present themselves." We commit ourselves "to Jesus Christ in union with the church, which Christ has opened to people of all ages, nations, and races."[13] Baptism is the ritual that marks our entry into a life of Christian discipleship. Long after our own baptism, each time we witness the baptism of others, we renew our own commitment to Christ through the words of the baptismal liturgy.

The meaning of Holy Communion is closely linked to the meaning of baptism. Whereas in baptism we are liturgically reborn through water, thus marking our birth as followers of Jesus, in Holy Communion we identify with Jesus's surrender of his life to the Father for the sake of the world. We commit to die to ourselves so as to live for Christ, again. In receiving into ourselves the bread and wine, we liturgically receive the very life of Christ, which nourishes us for the mission. The daily dying to ourselves is sometimes called everyday martyrdom, or daily martyrdom.

13. *UM Hymnal*, 33–44.

Dietrich Bonhoeffer, who himself later became a martyr under the Third Reich, wrote in his classic text *The Cost of Discipleship*, "When Christ calls a man, he bids him come and die."[14] The connection becomes obvious when we look at the Communion liturgy. Each time we partake of the bread and wine, we confess and renounce our sin, state our intent to follow Jesus, and commit ourselves to live in union with Christ and his mission. During the *epiclesis*, or the invocation of the Holy Spirit, we pray,

> Pour out your Holy Spirit on us gathered here, and on these gifts of bread and wine. Make them be for us the body and blood of Christ, that we may be for the world the body of Christ, redeemed by his blood. By your Spirit make us one with Christ, one with each other, and one in ministry to all the world, until Christ comes in final victory, and we feast at his heavenly banquet.[15]

Drawing from the metaphor of the bread and wine of the Lord's Supper, in his beautiful meditation *Life of the Beloved*, Henri J. M. Nouwen describes four movements in the Christian life.[16] We are taken, blessed, broken, and given. That is, we are gathered together into a community, or as I often say when presiding at Communion, we are diverse people gathered by God the Baker into something like a multigrain loaf. God kneads us into one loaf—blessing us, forgiving us of our sins, and setting us on a path of healing and reconciliation. At the benediction, God "breaks" the loaf of our community into many pieces by sending us forth to embody Jesus in the neighborhoods from which we come. In this way we become the Communion bread that God

---

14. Dietrich Bonhoeffer, *The Cost of Discipleship* (New York: Touchstone, 1995), 89.

15. *UM Hymnal*, 14.

16. Henri J. M. Nouwen, *Life of the Beloved: Spiritual Living in a Secular World* (New York: Crossroad, 2014).

gives to the world. The word becomes flesh and blood in us and moves into many neighborhoods.

Nouwen's theological vision is based upon the powerful scriptural truth that we are God's beloved (1 John 3:1). God loves us before we know how to love God. Just as God spoke to Jesus at his baptism, God speaks to us today: "You are my beloved child. With you I am well pleased" (see Mark 1:11). God's love binds us to God forever. In the embodied prayer of Holy Communion, we remember, we celebrate, and we commit ourselves to full participation in the mission of God.

Questions for Reflection

1. How does the connection between the theology of baptism and Communion described in this section compare to your experience or observation of these sacraments?

2. Reflect upon the missional nature of baptism and Communion. How might this central aspect of these holy celebrations be made clearer to the church when celebrating the sacraments?

3. Some people approach Holy Communion as a sorrowful liturgical moment in which the church remembers Christ's betrayal, suffering, and death. When you think of the idea of the faith community being "one loaf" that is taken, blessed, broken, and given, how might that metaphor change, deepen, or challenge the idea of Communion as a sorrowful experience?

John Wesley, the founder of Methodism, believed that Christians should partake of Communion as often as possible. In his sermon "The Duty of Constant Communion," Wesley argues that sharing at the Lord's table enables us to leave our sins behind and live as holy people. He makes a strong argument that daily Communion was the way of the early church and thus should be the pattern of contemporary Christians. Most of the sermon is a rebuttal of usual excuses Wesley's contemporaries gave for avoiding Communion.

In order to prepare for Communion, he teaches, Christians should truly wish to follow the commandments of God and to receive all the promises of God. One of the notable aspects of the Methodist faith and practice is "the open table," or the practice of inviting any and all who wish to partake to come. The liturgy issues this invitation: "Christ our Lord invites to his table all who love him, who earnestly repent of their sin, and seek to live in peace with one another."[17] Wesley believed that even if persons did not know Christ, they could come to know Christ's salvation in the act of Holy Communion if their hearts longed to know him and they came to the table with that hunger. In that case the table would be the first location of the genuinely Christian practice of celebration.

In her memoir *Take This Bread: A Radical Conversion*, Sara Miles tells the story of her extremely unlikely conversion while walking unexpectedly into St. Gregory of Nyssa Episcopal Church and to the Communion table.[18] Miles, a cynical forty-six-year-old war correspondent, experienced exactly what Methodists believe the Lord's Supper can do when the table is open to all. The Lord's Supper became the means of grace that welcomed Miles into the Christian faith and revealed her new vocation to her. At the table

17. *UM Hymnal*, 12.
18. Sara Miles, *Take This Bread: A Radical Conversion* (New York: Ballantine, 2008).

Miles underwent a Damascus Road[19] experience in which God showed her that the real meaning of Christianity is to feed the hungry, both spiritually and literally. Subsequently, she went to seminary and was ordained as an Episcopal priest, becoming active in the extraordinary food ministries of Gregory of Nyssa. Snarky, sometimes profane, and powerfully grounded in the gospel, Miles has become a prophetic voice of reform for the mainline church.

Holy Communion is a potent, embodied prayer of celebration through which we align ourselves fully with God's work of making all things new. Each time we eat the bread and drink the cup, we say "yes" to all that Christ is and all that he invites us to be, together. One of the earliest hymns of the church focuses on the union of the church with Christ in his way of being in the world:

> Let the same mind be in you that was in Christ Jesus,
>> who, though he was in the form of God,
>> did not regard equality with God
>> as something to be exploited,
> but emptied himself,
>> taking the form of a slave,
>> being born in human likeness.
> And being found in human form,
>> he humbled himself
>> and became obedient to the point of death—
>> even death on a cross.
> Therefore God also highly exalted him
>> and gave him the name
>> that is above every name,
> so that at the name of Jesus
>> every knee should bend,
>> in heaven and on earth and under the earth,

---

19. The apostle Paul encountered the living Christ on the Damascus Road, shattering all his former certainty about God and converting him to the faith he once persecuted. For the story of Paul's conversion, see Acts 9.

and every tongue should confess
    that Jesus Christ is Lord,
      to the glory of God the Father. (Philippians 2:5-11)

The Greek word for "emptied himself" is *kenosis*. It means to give oneself to others. This hymn is one of the most important passages of Scripture for the church today, calling the church to repent of the ways in which we have not loved our neighbors and have not taken the role of servant among our neighbors. Too often our posture toward those who are not in the church has been one of censure, judgment, or animosity. We do not see such attitudes or behaviors in Jesus in the Gospel narratives. The reason that every knee shall bow and every tongue confess that Jesus Christ is Lord is not that Jesus and his followers will take the world with violence or will shame and terrify the world into submission. Rather, the world comes to trust in Jesus's love when it experiences the church living in the way of Jesus, the way of kenosis. Celebrating through Holy Communion can help us to do that.

The Communion hymn "O Thou Who This Mysterious Bread"[20] is Charles Wesley's prayer that the risen Christ will be revealed through bread and wine in the same way he was revealed to the disciples on the walk to Emmaus (Luke 24:13-35). Although the resurrected Jesus walked and talked with the two disciples, they were unable to recognize him because their perception was blinded by grief over his death. Only when he agreed to stay and eat with them and blessed the meal were their eyes opened. "Were not our hearts burning within us while he was talking to us on the road, while he was opening the scriptures to us?" they asked each other afterward (verse 32). Propelled by overwhelming joy, they

20. *UM Hymnal,* no. 613.

left that same evening, hurrying back to Jerusalem to tell others the good news of Christ's resurrection.

Through the sacrament of Holy Communion, John Wesley urges Christians to open ourselves to receive the blessings that God offers and to commit ourselves to obey all God's commands. The word *obedience* is not popular in the church today, especially because historically it has been misused by those in power to oppress and subjugate women, children, people of color, and ethnic minorities, all in the name of God. However, the word comes from the Latin *oboedire*, which means "listening that leads to action." As we celebrate Communion, may we come with open hearts and minds, listening and ready to receive what God so lovingly offers. At the table, in the bread and cup, we encounter Jesus, who says to us, "I am here for you. Are you here for me?"

Questions for Reflection

1. Reflect upon the definition of *obedience* as "listening that leads to action." How is this meaning different from or similar to your previous experiences or understandings of obedience? What difference does this meaning make to the life of a faith community who hopes to practice Christian celebration as a way of being?

2. In this section, you read about the practice of an open Communion table within Methodism. How is a theology of an open table similar to or different from Communion experiences or teachings you have had?

3. How might celebrating Holy Communion help us to live in the way of Jesus that is "kenotic," or self-giving? In what way is the kenotic life an ongoing life of celebration?

Pilgrimage

As we continue to reflect on ways to celebrate through re-membering our own story and bringing it into God's story, we cannot help but turn to the ancient practice of making a spiritual pilgrimage. This type of journey is rugged because it is intended to facilitate spiritual transformation. While most spiritual pilgrimages have an important geographic destination such as Jerusalem, Iona, or Selma, the journey itself is what often brings about deep change.

I have had the privilege of coleading a number of pilgrimages to Scotland and England where we focus on Celtic Christian monastic spirituality. At Holy Island Lindisfarne and on Iona we pray, share meals and adventures together, learn about the Celtic saints and traditions, and have plenty of time for solitude. Unfailingly these experiences in the Iona Abbey and other sacred sites become transformational for ourselves and other pilgrims. Yet some of the most pivotal moments have happened when we had to face a problem of some kind with the journey.

One time a few years ago, nearly everyone's luggage was lost on the flight from the United States to the United Kingdom. We were scheduled to walk the Way of St. Cuthbert, a 62.5-mile walk from Melrose, Scotland, to Holy Island. The luggage didn't arrive until we had walked most of the way. While the lost luggage created enormous frustration and some hardship, it opened a "loaves and fish"[21] path for people to share what they did have

---

21. The story of the loaves and fish is found in Matthew 15:32-39 and Mark 8:1-9. In this story a boy shares his lunch of a few loaves of bread and some fish with the hungry disciples and Jesus, who miraculously multiplies it into enough food for a large crowd of several thousand people. The story illustrates what happens when people generously share what they have in times of need.

(socks, aspirin, T-shirts), experience genuine hospitality from one another, and learn how to travel with less. The depth of community that formed on that pilgrimage was more attributable to the lost luggage than to any of the sacred sites we visited!

One of the most profound pilgrimage experiences I have had took place in Oklahoma. I took a group of theology students there to experience pilgrimage focusing on Christianity and Cultures of the Plains Tribes. Dr. David Wilson, a member of the Choctaw Nation and an ordained pastor and superintendent in The United Methodist Church, facilitated the daily experiences we had, which included visiting sites where massacres had taken place, eating with a small Kiowa church where we heard traditional hymns in Kiowa, listening to a lecture from a Cherokee attorney whose work focuses on human rights on reservations, visiting the Oklahoma History Center to learn about the dreadful history of forced migration and genocide of hundreds of Native American tribes across North America, and participating in a sweat lodge led by a Native American Christian. The experience was theologically and emotionally disorienting for students whose education in American history had not included the Trail of Tears, the Indian Removal Act of 1830, or the military massacres of innocent people at Sand Creek, Washita, and many other places. This experience challenged students' theology of evangelism and mission and raised powerful questions of justice for marginalized indigenous people everywhere. That was a pilgrimage of pain and awakening that continues to bear fruit in many of those former students' lives as well as my own. By entering into Native American people's stories and experiencing the hospitality, memories, and wisdom of our hosts, our understanding of the gospel deepened in important ways. Our own stories changed because of that.

The spirituality and five essential disciplines of pilgrimage provide rich resources for the Christian practice of celebration, long after the pilgrimage experience is over. Pilgrimage becomes a way of being in the world that is deeply consistent with many other spiritual disciplines that foster a holy life.

The five core elements of pilgrimage include the following:

1. Pilgrimage is inherently disorienting. We intentionally leave what is familiar in God's care while moving forward with God toward what lies ahead. The disorientation of pilgrimage is what opens us for transformation.

2. Pilgrimage decenters us from ourselves and recenters us on God. Therefore, pilgrimage spirituality fosters humility and wonder, keeping heart and mind open to God. With this openness comes a teachability that then results in much celebration as we encounter God in ever-increasing ways.

3. Pilgrimage is hard work physically, emotionally, and spiritually. It is not a vacation or a tourist experience. Pilgrims learn to travel lightly, literally, to help with endurance and minimize potential for injury. The simplicity of traveling lightly becomes a posture for all of life, helping us to be content with enough and to resist excess.

4. Pilgrimage is full of surprises. Transformative encounters with God often come unexpectedly through moments of frustration, struggle, and pain. A spirituality of pilgrimage teaches us to look at the setbacks in life as opportunities to learn and grow rather than seethe with resentment.

5. Pilgrimage can become a habitual attitude as we mature spiritually. Upon completion of a pilgrimage such as a journey to Iona, Selma, Oklahoma, or Asissi, it is

important to intentionally take time for "reentry" to everyday life. That is, plan for and engage in a structured process that helps with naming and reflecting upon the gifts and challenges we experienced. In this way the spirituality of pilgrimage may remain with us and help us as the story of our lives continues to unfold.

Questions for Reflection

1. Have you ever experienced a pilgrimage? If so, where did you go? What did you experience? How were you changed by it, if at all? If you have not been on pilgrimage but one day had an opportunity to go, where would you go? Why are you drawn to that particular pilgrimage?

2. What kind of impact might it have on a congregation if the culture of the congregation was shaped by pilgrimage spirituality? How might this influence a congregation's capacity for celebration?

3. Transformation on a pilgrimage is more about the journey than the destination. People experience this reality in different ways. Describe a time in your life when you were on a journey of any kind in which you experienced transformation by what happened during the journey. This could be an inward journey or an outward journey or both.

Conclusion

Sometimes due to suffering, illness, loss, or trauma, we lose the capacity to celebrate God in our story. At those times others can celebrate with and for us. This was the case when we held a funeral for Bruce. Despite my bumbling efforts and the family's frustration, we did raise an Ebenezer that became more and more meaningful to the family as the years went by. We can be sure that at such times God is still for us and with us and is determined to make all things new. Our hampered capacity to celebrate does not diminish God's love for us. On the contrary, God comes to save us—to heal, forgive, and make new—precisely because we need divine help. And in coming for us, God adopts us into the divine story, which has a past, present, and future:

> So if anyone is in Christ, there is a new creation: everything old has passed away; see, everything has become new! All this is from God, who reconciled us to himself through Christ, and has given us the ministry of reconciliation; that is, in Christ God was reconciling the world to himself, not counting their trespasses against them, and entrusting the message of reconciliation to us. (2 Corinthians 5:17-19)

As we come to the end of this chapter focusing on memory, let's return to "Come, Thou Fount of Every Blessing," the hymn referenced earlier, based upon the story of Samuel raising an Ebenezer. Robert Robinson penned the lyrics to this hymn when he was just twenty-two years old. Having wandered from his faith in the manner of the prodigal son, Robinson came under the influence of fiery preacher George Whitefield and returned to his Baptist faith.[22] Three years after his conversion under Whitefield, Robinson wrote this hymn. Though an unlettered man, Robinson was a powerful preacher through whose ministry many

22. C. Michael Hawn, "History of Hymns: Come, Thou Fount of Every Blessing," https://www.umcdiscipleship.org/resources/history-of-hymns-come-thou-fount-of-every-blessing.

people found faith in Christ. In this hymn he celebrates God's love, mercy, and grace throughout his story. Each time we sing this song, we do the same.

> Come, thou Fount of every blessing,
> tune my heart to sing thy grace;
> streams of mercy, never ceasing,
> call for songs of loudest praise.
> Teach me some melodious sonnet,
> sung by flaming tongues above.
> Praise the mount! I'm fixed upon it,
> mount of thy redeeming love.
>
> Here I raise mine Ebenezer;
> hither by thy help I'm come;
> and I hope, by thy good pleasure,
> safely to arrive at home.
> Jesus sought me when a stranger,
> wandering from the fold of God;
> he, to rescue me from danger,
> interposed his precious blood.
>
> O to grace how great a debtor,
> daily I'm constrained to be!
> Let thy goodness, like a fetter,
> bind my wandering heart to thee.
> Prone to wander, Lord, I feel it,
> prone to leave the God I love;
> here's my heart, O take and seal it,
> seal it for thy courts above.[23]

---

23. *UM Hymnal*, no. 400.

Chapter Three
Failure

Helping people to embrace failure is one of the most important tasks in pioneering new forms of ministry. Though it doesn't feel like it at the time, failure can be our friend and wisdom teacher. Without our teacher, failure, none of us would have learned to ride a bicycle, read, play a musical instrument, cook, play sports, or experience intimacy. Yet in the church, it is often very difficult for someone who tries something new and fails simply to learn from the error and become more skilled. Grace toward other kinds of failure is even harder to come by. Rare is the Christian community that encourages its members to risk, fail, learn, and grow without shame in ministry and in life. Most of us have been in situations in the church where we proposed an idea for something creative or new, especially in order to reach out to neighbors beyond the church, only to be shut down by a curmudgeon who said, "We tried that once, and it didn't work. We'll never try anything like that again!" It is almost unheard of for congregations to practice the discipline of celebration as a response to failure.

The common posture within and beyond the church, of loathing toward self and others who fail, is based in fear and shame. Fear of failure suffocates the creative energy of the congregation and individuals. The shame of failure keeps people from being authentic with one another. In stark contrast, the practice of celebration in the face of failure gives people permission to learn and grow, to make mistakes—in short, to be human. Celebration after failure can go far to heal toxic shame, which then liberates individuals and congregations for joyous living.

Toxic shame is one of the most powerful, debilitating emotions we can experience. It is different from healthy shame, which helps us realize we made a mistake and need to do something about it. An example of healthy shame is "I am so dismayed because I got busy and forgot to pick up my daughter after school. She sat there for a half hour before I remembered. Next time I will make sure to set an alarm." (A real example, by the way, from my own years of mothering young children!) Healthy shame prods us to change our ways and make better choices in the future.

Toxic shame is the underlying conviction not that I *made* a mistake but that I *am* a mistake. I am inherently defective. I will never be good enough. I will never belong anywhere. I will always be on the outside looking in. These feelings are deeper than words, lodged in the marrow of our bones. But they give rise to incessant negative self-talk that can be triggered by almost anything. Toxic shame is a combination of embarrassment and grief and includes a sense of alienation and a need to hide either literally or in some symbolic way. Radiohead's 1992 hit song "Creep" perfectly captures the emotions of shame: "I'm a creep.... I don't belong here."[1]

One of the most common and pervasive aftereffects of abuse, especially sexual abuse, is toxic shame. Repeated experiences of workplace, school, or internet bullying based on gender, race, religion, body size, sexual identity, or other personal traits can lead to toxic shame. Societal shaming by the dominant "in" group toward other people reflected in systemic racism, sexism, homophobia, xenophobia, and more can create toxic shame when internalized by individuals from the "out" group. This kind of shame both drives and is the result of many addictions and other self-sabotaging behaviors and can sometimes lead to suicide.

Many of us grew up in shame-based families, including alcoholic families, drug-addicted families, toxically religious families, and workaholic families. While it is beyond the scope of this book to discuss in detail all the causes of shame, its manifestations, and what it takes to heal from shame, suffice to say that it is one of the most debilitating psychological forces with which many of us must contend on our way to shalom.[2] Often people who are bound by shame find that their greatest fear is fear of failure. The healing of this kind of shame is a major turning point in their lives, freeing them to risk and learn from life's inevitable mistakes.

Key

1.   Written by Mike Hazlewood, Albert Hammond, Colin Greenwood, Jonathan Greenwood, Edward O'Brien, Philip Selway, Thomas Yorke. Lyrics © Sony/ATV Music Publishing LLC, Warner Chappell Music, Inc, BMG Rights Management. You can listen to the entire song on YouTube at https://www.youtube.com/watch?v=XFkzRNyygfk. (Be aware that the song has some strong language.)

2.   For good book and video resources on healing from shame, I recommend John Bradshaw's work, which may be found at this website: http://www.john bradshaw.com/healingtheshamethatbindsyou1hourlecture.aspx. Another fine resource is the work of Brene Brown, a social scientist whose work focuses on shame. See www.brenebrown.com.

The healing of shame includes reframing one's own experience of failure as a normal and helpful part of human life, something that can foster important growth.[3] Some people refer to this practice as self-compassion.[4] If we can help one another view failure and error as useful teachers, we will not only be more humble, gracious, and compassionate toward ourselves when we fail, but we will also be able to help ourselves and help one another gain wisdom through failure. We will be able to celebrate.

Finally, we will not "take ourselves too seriously." A friend recently told me that she regretted she had spent most of her life taking herself too seriously and is now in recovery from that bad habit. We began talking about the expression in order to explore what *too seriously* actually means. What we discovered is that a person who takes herself too seriously is shame-bound because she cannot afford, emotionally or spiritually, to fail. She lives in continual, perfectionistic vigilance against making a mistake. Anxiety is her constant companion. When she does make a mistake, despite the compassion and empathy of those around her, she punishes herself mercilessly with internal self-criticism. At the end of our discussion my friend laughed and said, "But that was then. With God's help and a good therapist, I'm free at last!"

3. The discussion of shame and failure, above, is excerpted and used with permission from Elaine A. Heath and Larry Duggins, *Missional. Monastic. Mainline* (Eugene, OR: Cascade, 2014).

4. Kristin Neff, for example, is an expert on mindful self-compassion. Her professional research and personal experience as the mother of a child with autism give her a unique and compelling voice. See Krisiten Neff and Christopher Germer, "The Transformative Effects of Mindful Self-Compassion," January 19, 2019, https://www.mindful.org/the-transformative-effects-of-mindful-self-compassion/.

[handwritten: Don't remember / Attempt teach failure / being supportive]

Questions for Reflection

1. Describe a time you experienced failure as a child. What happened? How did you feel? How did people around you respond? *[handwritten: Embarrassed / Couldn't remember / Dumb]* *[handwritten: 4th grade — trying to teach fractions to class as I already had training in ed.]*

2. Describe a time as an adult when you failed at something but found it to be an important learning experience. What happened? How did you feel at the time? How did others around you respond? What are your thoughts and feelings about that experience now that you have some distance from it? What have you learned from the experience?

3. Think about your congregation or group of spiritual friends. If you as a faith community were not afraid of failure, what are some courageous or creative actions you would take? How can you help one another as a community to live into the freedom to fail? *[handwritten: teach! visiting ministry]* *[handwritten: Be Supportive! Invite people to try]*

4. I described a friend who healed from "taking herself too seriously." What might it mean for a faith community to "take itself too seriously"? How might that posture affect the life and practice of the community? What are some ways a congregation could heal from "taking itself too seriously"?

The Wrong People

One of the best stories in the New Testament that illustrate celebration in the face of moral failure is the call of Levi, the tax collector. This account also demonstrates why celebration in the face of failure is a prophetic act that most of us resist.

Jesus went out and saw a tax collector named Levi sitting at a kiosk for collecting taxes. Jesus said to him, "Follow me." Levi got up, left everything behind, and followed him. Then Levi threw a great banquet for Jesus in his home. A large number of tax collectors and others sat down to eat with them. The Pharisees and their legal experts grumbled against his disciples. They said, "Why do you eat and drink with tax collectors and sinners?" Jesus answered, "Healthy people don't need a doctor, but sick people do. I didn't come to call righteous people but sinners to change their hearts and lives." (Luke 5:27-32 CEB)

We can only imagine the horrified expressions on the disciples' faces when Jesus walked right up to Levi and invited him to join Jesus's merry band of friends. Levi was the ultimate traitor—to the disciples and every other Jew in the world. As a tax collector, Levi (whose name, ironically, is that of the priestly tribe) was in collusion with a corrupt system of taxation in Roman-occupied Palestine. Not only did he charge the high taxes demanded by the hated Roman government, Levi padded the amount so he could pocket the extra. If anyone refused to pay, Levi had soldiers near at hand to help with persuasion. He had become very wealthy in just this way. And everyone knew it. To invite Levi to the inner circle was to invite the enemy to their table.

Amazingly, Levi immediately "left everything behind." Not only did he leave everything at the kiosk, he permanently walked away from a life of comfort and privilege to follow an impoverished itinerant rabbi. Without Roman muscle to protect him, Levi now became an easy target for all those people he had cheated. To his dependents and most of his colleagues, Levi's conversion would have been seen as a colossal fail. From a spiritual perspective, however, the opposite was true. Levi's entire life until that time had been a fail.

The first thing Levi wanted to do was celebrate. In no time, Levi invited everyone he could think of to meet Jesus by throwing a huge party. No expense was spared. Levi was overjoyed with his new beginning and ready to introduce all his friends to Jesus. Levi became an evangelist to all his friends and associates, just as the Samaritan woman did when she evangelized her village.[5] The Bible is filled with stories of God choosing "the wrong people." Jesus loves to choose "the wrong people" to be his ambassadors in the world. People like Levi. People with a checkered past.

As always, Jesus's critics showed up and wasted no time in lobbing insults. "Why are you always eating with tax collectors and sinners?" they complained. The irony is wondrous. We can imagine them biting into one of the little sandwiches at the buffet table while they make their complaint. After all, they also showed up for dinner with "those people"!

In Mark's account of this story, Jesus sits down to eat with Levi's guests, "many of [whom] had become his followers" (Mark 2:15b CEB). Could it be that some of Levi's friends who had become followers of Jesus had paved the way for Levi to be ready for Jesus's invitation? Matthew tells the same story but includes these words from Jesus as he responded to the criticism about eating with the wrong people: "Go and learn what this means: *I want mercy and not sacrifice.* I didn't come to call righteous people, but sinners" (Matthew 9:13 CEB).[6]

In those two brief sentences, we discover the central reason for Christian celebration. Jesus comes to us not because we are

5. The story of the Samaritan woman at the well is found in John 4.
6. In Matthew's account the tax collector is named Matthew. Traditionally, Matthew and Levi are thought to be the same person.

good or impressive or make all the right choices. On the contrary, Jesus reaches out to us in the midst of our own colossal fails, especially what we call "moral failure." Just as Jesus did with Levi, Jesus marches straight up to our own version of a tax collector's booth, whether that is a string of divorces, lifelong greed, a history of bullying, or an identity forged in our betrayal of others. "Come and follow me," Jesus says. He does not shame us, threaten us, or recite a long list of what is wrong with us. We have already done that to ourselves. We have lived for what seems forever with the constant voice of shame. Instead, Jesus invites us into the fellowship of his closest friends where a new day, a new life can emerge.

We just make sin!
Confess our failures.

Questions for Reflection

1. How does the shame of failure keep us from being authentic with one another in our faith communities? How can we help our faith community move into greater authenticity? What will be some of the outcomes?

2. Why do people automatically think of sexual sin when they hear the term "moral failure"? What does this assumption say about us and our values? Make a list of other kinds of moral failure. How might an experience of moral failure also become a teacher that helps us grow?

unethical
amoral
setting self lst.

3. Jesus says in Matthew's account of Levi's call, "*I want mercy and not sacrifice.*" Mercy is actually a type of sacrifice. What is sacrificed when we practice mercy? Does being merciful automatically lead to being "soft on sin," or complicit with sinful behaviors? Why does Jesus want mercy and not sacrifice? Why do we resist mercy?

4. How is the practice of mercy also a practice of celebration?

Failure, Sin, Mercy, and Celebration

In his book *The Wounded Heart of God*, theologian Andrew Sung Park describes the God who wants mercy more than sacrifice. According to Park, God is our loving Creator who sees humans not first and foremost as *sinners* but as those who were first *sinned against*. We are sinned against before we ever sin. We are born into a world where brokenness already exists and will inevitably wound us. Or to draw from the Creation stories of Genesis 1–3, every one of us is born into a garden with a lying snake.[7] We will inevitably be sinned against, and out of those experiences and their aftermath, we will inevitably become people who sin. God sees this reality with compassion and a commitment to act on our behalf. God is for us.

God looks at us through a heart of mercy that takes into account our entire story from conception to the current time and the entire history of wounds, sin, and salvation in our family, community, and neighborhood that make up the fabric of our social context. Drawing from the Korean philosophical concept of *han*, Park offers a compelling vision of salvation as the healing of wounds and their residue in our lives, both on individual and communal levels. Han, he explains, "is a deep, unhealed wound of a victim that festers in her or him. It can be a social, economic, political, physical, or spiritual wound generated by political oppression, economic exploitation, social alienation, cultural contempt, injustice, poverty, or war."[8] Moreover, han is experienced by victims of sexual abuse, partner violence, neglect and violence

---

7. I have written in detail elsewhere about Genesis 3 as a story of Adam and Eve being sinned against by the serpent. See *Healing the Wounds of Sexual Abuse: Reading the Bible with Survivors* (Grand Rapids: Brazos, 2019).

8. Andrew Sung Park, *Triune Atonement: Christ's Healing for Sinners, Victims, and the Whole Creation* (Louisville: Westminster John Knox, 2009), 39.

from parents, bullying, and many other forms of degradation. Han develops when victims are "boxed in," unable to grieve and find release from what has happened.[9] In short, han is the crippling residue left from experiencing harm. It is the source of many dysfunctional behaviors that develop as coping mechanisms.

In his landmark work *The Body Keeps the Score*, psychologist Bessel Van der Kolk describes the way that trauma lodges in the body, not just in memories or thoughts. The healing of trauma requires attending to the way the body holds trauma so that the body can return to a state of rest.[10] Significant parallels exist between the healing of han and the healing of trauma. In both cases essential healing practices include the presence of empathetic listeners; participation in a safe community of friends where one truly knows and is known by others; and reintegration of body, mind, emotions, and spirituality through mindfulness, exercise, play, singing, and other activities.

As we think about the many stories in the Bible in which Jesus calls people like Levi—public sinners who are held in contempt by their community because of their moral failure—we can see how Jesus not only forgives their sin but heals their han. He does this through words, listening, physical touch, respect, invitation to a shared meal, and welcoming "the despised other" into his circle of friends. This pattern of deep transformation is clear in the healing of the Samaritan woman at the well (John 4:4-42) and the call of Zacchaeus (Luke 19:1-10). One of the most beautiful stories of forgiveness and the healing of han in the New Testament takes place at a dinner where Jesus is eating with a mixed group of friends and critics:

---

9. Park, *Triune Atonement*, 40.
10. Bessel Van der Kolk, *The Body Keeps the Score* (New York: Penguin, 2014), 2–4.

One of the Pharisees asked Jesus to eat with him, and he went into the Pharisee's house and took his place at the table. And a woman in the city, who was a sinner, having learned that he was eating in the Pharisee's house, brought an alabaster jar of ointment. She stood behind him at his feet, weeping, and began to bathe his feet with her tears and to dry them with her hair. Then she continued kissing his feet and anointing them with the ointment. Now when the Pharisee who had invited him saw it, he said to himself, "If this man were a prophet, he would have known who and what kind of woman this is who is touching him—that she is a sinner." Jesus spoke up and said to him, "Simon, I have something to say to you." "Teacher," he replied, "speak." "A certain creditor had two debtors; one owed five hundred denarii, and the other fifty. When they could not pay, he canceled the debts for both of them. Now which of them will love him more?" Simon answered, "I suppose the one for whom he canceled the greater debt." And Jesus said to him, "You have judged rightly." Then turning toward the woman, he said to Simon, "Do you see this woman? I entered your house; you gave me no water for my feet, but she has bathed my feet with her tears and dried them with her hair. You gave me no kiss, but from the time I came in she has not stopped kissing my feet. You did not anoint my head with oil, but she has anointed my feet with ointment. Therefore, I tell you, her sins, which were many, have been forgiven; hence she has shown great love. But the one to whom little is forgiven, loves little." Then he said to her, "Your sins are forgiven." But those who were at the table with him began to say among themselves, "Who is this who even forgives sins?" And he said to the woman, "Your faith has saved you; go in peace." (Luke 7:36-50)

Jesus recognized the woman's lavish attentiveness as an act of worshipful celebration for how Jesus had forgiven and welcomed her. Jesus did not sexualize her intent the way his host Simon did, but Jesus saw her heart. He reframed her actions to judgmental onlookers, honoring her for her generosity and hospitality. He received her nurturing (if unusual) touch in the spirit in which it was given. All of these actions "unboxed" the woman from her stuck place in society and enabled her to begin her life anew.

Questions for Reflection

1. How is this discussion of salvation as forgiveness of sin and the healing of han similar to or different from what you have learned in the past about sin and salvation?

2. Using a meditative reading of Scripture, reread the story of the sinful woman described in this section. Read slowly, imagining that you are one of the Pharisees at the table. What do you see, hear, smell, taste, feel, wonder, and think? Now read it again from the perspective of a disciple of Jesus. What do you see, hear, smell, taste, feel, wonder, and think? Read it a third time from the perspective of the woman. What do you see, hear, smell, taste, feel, wonder, and think?

3. Think about a time in your life when you experienced individual or collective harm that left residue, or han. In what ways has that han shaped your relationships with yourself, God, and others? Where are you in the healing process: waiting to start, early in the process, or well along the way? How have you experienced this discussion of han and sin in light of your own story? If you are waiting to start healing from han or early in the process, what might help you move forward?

4. Think about a time when someone truly forgave you for a mistake you made that caused you to fail that person in some way. How did you feel when you knew you were forgiven? How did you know you were truly forgiven and that it was not just a set of words spoken to you? How did you celebrate?

Clearing Us Out
for Some New Delight

When it began, we did not know The Great Exodus was underway. Our friends had told us many months before moving that they would not be able to continue to live in community with us. Due to age-related health challenges, the stairs in our home were becoming a safety hazard. The four of us were sad but understood that their move was necessary. As the day approached for their departure, we talked about the wonderful years we had shared a home and life and much ministry. We gave thanks for all the time we had together and rejoiced that after the move, they would only be a few miles away, living with their daughter and son-in-law, who are also our friends. We made plans to continue to meet regularly for meals and prayer, and we hoped to continue our shared ministries in spiritual formation and in leading retreats for others.

But within a few months after moving, their daughter got a new job in another city many miles away. Soon all four of them relocated to the new city. Weekly meals and prayers were not going to happen after all. Our shared ministry of spiritual formation and retreats abruptly came to an end. At the same time, I went through an unexpected job change. While my new institution did not require a geographic move for us, nonetheless the new circumstance launched a domino effect with other changes in relationships, resources, congregational connections, expectations for our community, finances, and plans for the future. While still adjusting to all those transitions, three more friends moved away, each for different reasons, some because of differing expectations of community. It felt as if our world had shifted on its axis. After ten years of living in community, my spouse and I found ourselves alone on a twenty-three-acre farm with two houses, twenty-five chickens, three ducks, and two dogs. It was after the last of our friends drove away that we named that season The Great Exodus.

As The Great Exodus unfolded and picked up speed, a line from Rumi's poem "The Guest House" began to repeat itself in my thoughts: "He may be clearing you out for some new delight."[11] In this poem Rumi likens daily life to running a guest house. As host it is important to greet and be grateful for each day's "guests," to throw open the door and laugh even if the visitors are mean thoughts and actions, even if they are "a crowd of sorrows" who sweep your house clean of everything familiar. Every guest holds the potential for divine guidance, leading us to something different and wonderful.

We definitely had our house swept clean by a crowd of sorrows. But I was not so sure that a new delight was around the corner. Instead, I found myself increasingly bracing for the next onslaught, whatever it might be.

Even as "clearing you out for some new delight" ran through my mind over and over, a tiny internal voice said, "Your community is a failure. You're a fraud. Pack it in." So it was that my primary spiritual work during The Great Exodus was to identify, name, and engage the accusing voice of toxic shame yet again. It was a guest that I had to welcome to the guest house so that I could see what triggered it and how I could heal at deeper levels while refusing to give that voice power over me. Welcoming and learning from the unpleasant guest did not mean I had to agree with it or give it the keys to the house. But welcoming the guest

---

11. Jelaluddin Rumi, "The Guest House," translated by Coleman Barks, copyright 1997, https://gratefulness.org/resource/guest-house-rumi/.

was part of celebrating God's wisdom coming to me even through unpleasant means.

My work was also to trust that there truly would be a new delight. Anticipatory celebration was not easy work. But in time the new delight began to emerge. Others came to join us in community, some in residence and others in close proximity. The new delight revealed itself through increasing numbers of children coming to learn, grow, play, garden, and worship with us. New opportunities surfaced for us to companion refugees. We began hosting monthly campfires that quickly took on a life of their own with laughter, hotdogs, and stories. This all happened organically over a period of a year. The new delight happened because of the wide open physical and spiritual space that resulted from the emptying of The Great Exodus. Celebration over what was emerging was indeed a joyous thing. We continue to celebrate what is rising.

But let's return to the matter of failure. What we experienced in The Great Exodus—the disbanding of a configuration of community in which we had lived for years—was not a matter of moral failure on anyone's part. It was more about a collision of difficult circumstances in all our lives that made it impossible to remain together in the same way.

One of the stressors was my seventy-hours-per-week job in which I had been hired to lead systems change in an institution that was not yet ready for such change. Before my appointment to that position, I had been much more present to our community and able to participate in many more activities because I had time and energy to invest in community life. With the change of employment to the administrative post, I no longer had that kind of time or energy. With my decreased participation in the community, understandably the dynamics of our house changed. Leaving the high-stress appointment was a welcome move, in no small part because it restored my time and energy for our community, but that transition also impacted all of us in complex and painful ways.

Some aspects of what felt like failure within our community had to do with a natural life cycle for a particular iteration of our intentional community. In that case the end of the residential community as it had existed wasn't so much a failure as it was reaching the end of a season because of health challenges. But the grief of separating felt like failure. Other aspects of failure during The Great Exodus had to do with people's differing expectations, histories, and limitations. Not everyone is ready or able to live in community over the long haul. And even those of us who are called to live in community sometimes need a season away. This is why in traditional monastic communities, some type of hermitage is usually available for occasional use.

Celebration was one of the practices that got us through the pain of The Great Exodus. Morning and evening prayer were times to call upon God, remember God's call upon us, and cast our cares upon the one who cares for us (1 Peter 5:7). Journaling helped me to notice what God was doing from week to week and to be honest with God about my struggles. Meals and conversations with trusted spiritual friends provided encouragement we needed to stay the course, to keep showing up and trusting God with our liminal space. Walks through the forest and around the farm and pausing several times per week to watch the sunset reminded us of God's faithfulness in creation. These small, frequent acts of celebration gave us strength to endure. On days we felt we had no more strength, God carried us. We learned anew what it means to belong to the Good Shepherd.

Questions for Reflection

1. Think about a time when you did what you believed to be your calling or your responsibility, but the outcome was not what you had hoped for. How did you feel? How did others around you respond to you? Who or what provided support for you as you moved through the disappointing feelings of failure?

2. Sometimes when relationships change over time, an end to the way things "used to be" can feel like a failure regardless of the reason. When have you experienced a changed relationship that caused you to wrestle with feelings of failure? How did you process what you were experiencing? Were there people or situations that helped you to celebrate God's faithfulness in the midst of painful change?

3. Read the poem "The Guest House," by Rumi, at https://gratefulness.org/resource/guest-house-rumi/. Spend time reflecting on the themes of the poem. How does the poem encourage, challenge, confront, or confirm your perspectives about life? How is the posture recommended in "The Guest House" one of celebration?

4. This section describes the importance of walking through field and forest and watching the sunset as means of celebrating God's faithfulness during uncertain days. Where might you go in order to be present to creation as a means of celebration in your own life?

Chapter Three

Why Did This Happen?

Sometimes failure is the outcome of doing the right thing, of answering God's call, of being faithful. To fail at such times can be so confusing and disheartening. When I have such experiences, I tend to default to questions like these: Did I misunderstand God's leading? Did I miss the mark in discernment? Have I made a wrong choice? What did I do that caused this problem? Why did this happen? And on and on until finally I get down to root questions: What kind of God is God? Why would God either cause or allow this suffering to happen?

The Bible includes many stories about people who failed because of doing the right thing. Job comes to mind immediately. In Job's case, his massive losses of family, friends, resources, and public respect took place precisely *because* he was faithful. It all began when God boasted to Satan about Job's virtue. The setting was a divine court of law, so to speak:

> One day the heavenly beings came to present themselves before the Lord, and Satan also came among them. The Lord said to Satan, "Where have you come from?" Satan answered the Lord, "From going to and fro on the earth, and from walking up and down on it." The Lord said to Satan, "Have you considered my servant Job? There is no one like him on the earth, a blameless and upright man who fears God and turns away from evil." Then Satan answered the Lord, "Does Job fear God for nothing? Have you not put a fence around him and his house and all that he has, on every side? You have blessed the work of his hands, and his possessions have increased in the land. But stretch out your hand now, and touch all that he has, and he will curse you to your face." The Lord said to Satan, "Very well, all that he has is in your power; only do not stretch out your hand against him!" So Satan went out from the presence of the Lord. (Job 1:6-12)

Soon Satan struck Job with one calamity after another. In a matter of hours, Job lost his children and wealth to marauders, wildfire, wind, and war. Before long painful boils spread across his body, causing endless torment. The final indignities include the contempt of his wife, who urged him to "curse God, and die" (Job 2:9), and the judgments of his friends, who assumed Job must be guilty of sin. Job himself had some pointed questions for God. None of the actors in this drama knew what was really going on behind the scenes, which was that Satan was at work, trying to destroy Job's faith.

In the end Job recovered from his illness, with his fortunes restored and doubled. He had more children, his new set of daughters being the most beautiful women in the land. But before that happened, in a most satisfying turn of poetic justice, Job's friends had to repent. They were guilty of theological malfeasance. In their haste to explain away Job's suffering, they had presented a damning vision of God. So then they had to bring costly sacrifices and ask Job to preside over the ritual, interceding for them so that they would not experience the wrath of God that God said they truly deserved (Job 42). Job, who like his friends at one time had many ignorant words about God, now knew God, now had seen the mystery of God that is too deep for words (Job 42:5). He offered the sacrifice for his friends. He prayed for their forgiveness. It is at that point that his life was restored.

The genre of the book of Job is a drama in which both God and Job are "on trial." Many scholars think that Job is the oldest book in the Bible because of the style of writing and lack of references to Moses, the Law, and other narratives. As part of the collection of books of the Hebrew Bible known as Wisdom Literature, the overarching purpose of Job is to engender spiritual wisdom in its readers. Specifically, the Book of Job guides us through reflections on the spiritual torment and sense of failure that comes to faithful, God-loving people who don't get what they deserve. Instead, they experience what feels like punishment. The Book of Job is meant to succor us during our own experiences of inexplicable suffering and to prevent us from turning into Job's friends, full of ignorant, harmful, blasphemous words about God in the face of human suffering, adding to that suffering through our arrogance.

In the New Testament, we encounter many people who suffer for doing the right thing. None of them suffer more than the apostle Paul, whose story begins with his theological violence against Christians. We first meet Paul under his Hebrew name Saul[12] in Acts 7:58, where he was present for the stoning of the first Christian martyr: "Then they dragged him [Stephen] out of the city and began to stone him; and the witnesses laid their coats at the feet of a young man named Saul." We can imagine him standing just out of range of dust and blood, holding the executioners' garments to keep them tidy. That Saul approved of the murder is obvious from what happened next.

A great persecution breaks out immediately after the martyrdom of Stephen, with Saul leading the way. Ironically, though the disciples had been told by Jesus to wait for the Holy Spirit, who would empower them to go and be his witnesses around the world, after the Spirit was given, the disciples generally stayed put. They were still in Jerusalem when the great persecution began. Acts 8:3 records the vengeance of Saul against the perceived

---

12. The New Testament calls him by his Hebrew name, Saul, until he undergoes conversion to Christ. After that he is usually called Paul. As a Roman citizen he would have had three names—his Roman name (Paulus), his Hebrew name (Saul), and his family name, which is unknown.

threat of the new sect: "Saul was ravaging the church by entering house after house; dragging off both men and women, he committed them to prison." Scattered to many places, the persecuted disciples shared the gospel as they went. The promise of the Father that they would become a global witness finally began to be fulfilled, but not in a way they would have chosen.

Saul, "breathing threats and murder against the disciples of the Lord" is then authorized to track down the scattered disciples and bring them back to Jerusalem for prosecution (Acts 9:1-2). While on his way to Damascus, Saul is suddenly confronted by the risen Christ:

> Now as he was going along and approaching Damascus, suddenly a light from heaven flashed around him. He fell to the ground and heard a voice saying to him, "Saul, Saul, why do you persecute me?" He asked, "Who are you, Lord?" The reply came, "I am Jesus, whom you are persecuting. But get up and enter the city, and you will be told what you are to do." The men who were traveling with him stood speechless because they heard the voice but saw no one. Saul got up from the ground, and though his eyes were open, he could see nothing; so they led him by the hand and brought him into Damascus. For three days he was without sight, and neither ate nor drank.
>
> Now there was a disciple in Damascus named Ananias. The Lord said to him in a vision, "Ananias." He answered, "Here I am, Lord." The Lord said to him, "Get up and go to the street called Straight, and at the house of Judas look for a man of Tarsus named Saul. At this moment he is praying, and he has seen in a vision a man named Ananias come in and lay his hands on him so that he might regain his sight." But Ananias answered, "Lord, I have heard from many about this man, how much evil he has done to your saints in Jerusalem; and here he has authority from the chief priests to bind all who invoke your name." But the Lord said to him, "Go, for he is an instrument whom I have chosen to bring my name before Gentiles and kings and before the people of Israel; I myself will show him how much he must suffer for the sake of my name."

So Ananias went and entered the house. He laid his hands on Saul and said, "Brother Saul, the Lord Jesus, who appeared to you on your way here, has sent me so that you may regain your sight and be filled with the Holy Spirit." And immediately something like scales fell from his eyes, and his sight was restored. Then he got up and was baptized, and after taking some food, he regained his strength. (Acts 9:3-19)

Though he begins preaching about Christ in Damascus immediately upon recovery, unsurprising in light of his zealous nature, before long an attempt is made on his life by some of his former colleagues. Never one to shrink from danger, Paul returns to Jerusalem where he finds a friend in Barnabas, who welcomes him into the frightened remnant of Jesus followers who at this time are called the Way. Once again Paul has to flee for his own safety. The next time Paul is mentioned in Acts, Barnabas has come to Tarsus to retrieve him so that they can serve the church together in Antioch (Acts 11:26). It is during this time in Antioch under Paul and Barnabas's leadership that Jesus's followers begin to be called Christians, a term of derision that means "little Christs."

As Paul launched into his letter to the Galatians, he described the ego-shattering Damascus Road experience. In a long passage (Galatians 1:11–2:21), he provided a detailed narrative to persuade the Galatians that he had not come into a more expansive theology without great struggle.[13]

13. For an accessible to laypersons scholarly article about Paul's wilderness experiences, see N. T. Wright, "Paul, Arabia, and Elijah (Galatians 1:17)," *Journal of Biblical Literature*, vol. 115: 683–92; reprinted on N. T. Wright Page, http:// ntwrightpage.com/Wright_Paul_Arabia_Elijah.pdf. Scholars disagree on how to interpret the different versions of Paul's story that are found in Acts and Galatians. For a discussion of these differences see C. W. Hansen, "Letter to the Galatians," *Dictionary of Paul and His Letters*, ed. Gerald F. Hawthorne, Ralph P. Martin, and Daniel G. Reid (Downers Grove, IL: InterVarsity, 1993), 332–33.

Paul said that he was a violent man, advanced beyond others his age in his knowledge and zeal for tradition. (He was apparently following the violent Shammaite school of thought within the larger Pharisee tradition, carrying out his duty to use whatever means necessary to suppress theological deviance.) He was the ultimate defender of the faith, ruthless in his persecution of Christians. After his conversion and brief time in Damascus and Jerusalem, Paul journeyed to the wilderness of Arabia, which in his day was a vast and not clearly defined geographic area southeast of Palestine and, of particular importance, the location of Mount Sinai. That was where Moses was given the Law. It was the most holy place a devout Hebrew such as Paul could go in order to listen to God and come to terms with what had happened to him.[14] There, over a period of time, he experienced direct revelations from Jesus.

The content of those encounters radically changed how Paul understood his own Jewish tradition. He neither rejected nor disrespected his tradition but came to see it in a new light. Non-Jews are just as beloved to God as Jews, he realized. Following the rituals of the Hebrew tradition is not necessary for people to fully experience the love and salvation of God. Jesus the Messiah is for all people, not just for Hebrew people. The Jews have been given a special role of bringing the Messiah into the world for the whole world. All of these revelations dismantled what Paul previously thought he knew about God. Paul had also seen that his life would be marked with persecution, the same kind of trauma he once inflicted on others. In this passage Paul does not explain

14. N. T. Wright provides valuable insight on the parallels between Paul and Elijah in Paul's autobiographical narratives. Paul is deliberately reinforcing his own call as a prophet in the great tradition of Hebrew prophets. See Wright, "Paul, Arabia, and Elijah (Galatians 1:17)."

precisely how the revelations were given, whether by dream, vision, a visible encounter with the risen Christ, or contemplative awareness. He simply says he was given revelations of Jesus Christ.

The remainder of the Epistle to the Galatians is Paul's argument for the tradition behind his Hebrew tradition. Paul's heart had been captured by the love of Christ. He had surrendered to the authority of Christ. As a result, he had given himself completely to God's mission in the world, and it was a mission to everyone. As he says in Galatians 3:28, "There is no longer Jew or Greek, there is no longer slave or free, there is no longer male and female; for all of you are one in Christ Jesus." In this, his first epistle that was canonized, Paul subsumes his own tradition to the deeper, more ancient tradition of God making all things new. For the rest of his life Paul suffered for doing what was right, for faithfully following Jesus and participating in God's mission to all people.[15]

Public theological failure—the experience of Job's friends and of Paul—is one of the most humbling (or even humiliating) experiences for us pastors and theologians to experience. The need to be right, to have explanations, is powerful for religious leaders, ordained and lay alike. When our theology fails, when the rug is pulled out from under our theological legs by suffering, calamity, loss, cataclysm, or a hard awakening, we are finally rendered mute. We find ourselves in the dust, scratching our sores with a pottery shard while others look on in judgment (Job 2:8).

It is at that point that we either become bitter in our disillusionment or we return to childlike humility. The very word

---

15. The section on the life of Paul is excerpted and adapted from Elaine A. Heath, *God Unbound: Wisdom from Galatians for the Anxious Church* (Nashville: Upper Room, 2016), Kindle edition, location 205–65.

humble comes from the Latin root *humus,* or the decomposed plant and animal matter that is essential to soil health. As any good gardener knows, humus is the crucial building block for plants. Not only does humus provide nutrients, especially nitrogen, for plants but it also enables soil to retain moisture. Humus is the most important ingredient for healing soil that has been leached through overuse or abuse. Public theological failure produces humus for the soul. To fail theologically after being so very right for so many years, with power over so many people in those years, is to become grounded, open to the mystery of God and life, in touch with who God really is and what God is really up to in this world.

Questions for Reflection

1. In the story of Job, none of the characters ever learn why Job's faith was tested. They do not know about the courtroom scene, or Satan, or God's bet that Job will endure. Does their "unknowing" mirror a difficult and inexplicable experience you have had that continues to be a mystery? If so, how does it feel to you to read the story of Job at this time? What are the questions or insights that surface in your reflections?

2. Job's friends began well enough in sitting with Job as he began to suffer. But then things took a turn in their relationship with him. Why did this happen? Have you ever seen or experienced this kind of behavior either from others or within yourself in the face of inexplicable suffering?

3. Sometimes we think about life as if everyone gets what they deserve: God doles out blue skies and good health

to the faithful and disaster to those who sin. The stories of Job and Paul both contradict that idea. What else do the stories of Job and Paul have in common? How do Job and Paul learn to celebrate in the midst of their troubles?

4. Have you ever suffered for making the right choice, for following God's call, or for doing the right thing? What happened? How did you respond to the suffering? Were there people or was there internal strength that helped you to celebrate God's presence in the midst of your struggle? If not, what might have helped?

Conclusion

A few years ago, I participated in a Center for Teaching Excellence presentation with two faculty members from Southern Methodist University: a Cox School of Business professor and a physicist. I know, it sounds like a joke: "A theologian, an executive, and a physicist went into a bar . . ." We each did a presentation on how we strive for high-impact teaching. What the physicist Stephen Sekula said has stayed with me and deeply enriched my own perspectives on failure. Professor Sekula said that he teaches his students that science cannot move forward without a great deal of failure. Scientists as a matter of course risk trying big ideas, knowing most of those ideas will fail. But the failures are how they learn. Science moves forward by failing forward.

Recently our friends came walking down the driveway, huge grins on all their faces. "Guess what?" the children shouted. "Annalima started walking today!" I smiled at the adorable baby in her sister's arms, who stared back soberly. "Is this true, Annalima?" I asked. "I need to see for myself!" So Abigail put the baby down gently, turned her toward her mother who was a few yards away with outstretched arms, and said, "Go to Mommy!" Annalima fixed her eyes on her mother, let go of her sister's hands, and lurched wildly toward her mother's arms, stunned by her own power. The rest of us cheered and clapped. A celebration was in order. In another week or two Annalima would be unstoppable, because she is constantly failing forward, learning to stand, now learning to walk, soon learning to run.

Chapter Four

Celebration in a Divided World

In the first three chapters, we have given considerable attention to what it means to celebrate God's love, God's healing
and forgiving and liberating work, the salvation of the world.
We have thought about how to practice celebration in the midst
of spiritual fog, through the remembrance of stories with all their
pain and joy, and when we or others fail. As we journeyed through
these reflections, we came to see how deeply the practice of celebration is tied to our theology—that is, to what we actually love
and trust about God, how we actually pray, and how we inhabit
our own neighborhoods. Along the way we looked deeply into
our own stories and hearts to find the wisdom of the Holy Spirit
guiding us. Now we shall turn to what may be the most challenging and necessary form of celebration for us at this time, which is
to be a people of holy celebration in the midst of a divided world.
We live in a society fraught with violent divisions, and far too
often those fractures emanate from and divide the church.

That They May Be One

As Jesus prepared for his own death, he prayed for his disciples and all the people who would come to love and follow him throughout time.

> I ask not only on behalf of these, but also on behalf of those who will believe in me through their word, that they may all be one. As you, Father, are in me and I am in you, may they also be in us, so that the world may believe that you have sent me. The glory that you have given me I have given them, so that they may be one, as we are one, I in them and you in me, that they may become completely one, so that the world may know that you have sent me and have loved them even as you have loved me. Father, I desire that those also, whom you have given me, may be with me where I am, to see my glory, which you have given me because you loved me before the foundation of the world. Righteous Father, the world does not know you, but I know you; and these know that you have sent me. I made your name known to them, and I will make it known, so that the love with which you have loved me may be in them, and I in them. (John 17:20-26)

In this prayer, Jesus names the one sign and wonder that will convince our neighbors that the gospel is trustworthy and true. What is that sign and wonder? It is a public demonstration of the love that binds Jesus and the Father together, which now binds together all who love and follow Jesus. Whether we like it or not, whether we feel it or not, whether we know it or not, we are all bound together in Jesus's heart. To live in that truth is to present to our neighbors an alternative vision for life on planet earth, one in which all the old divisions caused by sin, all the phobias and isms attached to embodiment, geography, economic status, politics, and nationality, are healed. In our current situation, the vision of a community that models the new creation may seem like an impossible dream. Yet the new creation here, now, in our mortal lives and not just in heaven someday, is what the gospel is all about. Jesus has already shown us the way of transformation.

What is the method God has given for the transformation of the world? How do we do this? By living the great hymn of self-emptying that Paul quoted in his letter to the Philippians:

> Let the same mind be in you that was in Christ Jesus,
> who, though he was in the form of God,
> > did not regard equality with God
> > as something to be exploited,
> but emptied himself,
> > taking the form of a slave. (Philippians 2:5-7)

By becoming self-emptying communities of Jesus followers who live, work, and serve for the flourishing of our neighborhoods. By reflecting within our communities of faith the healing of every sinful division that fractures our society. By finally, for the first time in history, sustaining in real life the extraordinary vision that the apostle Paul described in his letter to the Galatians: "For in Christ Jesus you are all children of God through faith. As many of you as were baptized into Christ have clothed yourselves with Christ. There is no longer Jew or Greek, there is no longer slave or free, there is no longer male and female; for all of you are one in Christ Jesus" (Galatians 3:26-28).

God's way, the spiritual way, is simple but not easy. In order to cultivate the kind of community that Jesus prays for in John 17, we must die to many things. We have to give up—day by day, hour by hour, moment by moment—our little fiefdoms, our petty preferences, our exaggerations, our bigotry, our resistance to mercy, our vindictiveness, our craving for attention, our hiding from our own gifts and call, our narcissistic visions of church, our disrespect for ourselves and one another, our bland cooperation with whatever is easy, our laziness, our lack of self-awareness, our active and passive aggression, and our religious violence. There is so much more that could be said. Paul summed it up as "the works of the flesh," and by "flesh" he meant self-serving behavior that harms both self and others.[1]

The Greek word translated "flesh" is *sarx*, a multifaceted word that in this context means flawed human nature that is prone to wrong choices. Robert Robinson captured the meaning of sarx perfectly in the third stanza of "Come, Thou Fount of Every Blessing": "Prone to wander, Lord, I feel it, prone to leave the God I love."[2] What the world needs from the church in order to know that the gospel is true and real and worthy of their lives is for us Christians to own, name, and repent of our love of sarx and then to choose to be communities that answer Jesus's prayer in John 17. We must do this for the sake of our neighbors and for the sake of our own souls.

Questions for Reflection

1. What are the societal divisions that seem to be most pressing in your own neighborhood? your town or city?

2. In what ways does your faith community struggle with the fragmentation that is found in wider culture beyond the church? How does your faith community resist the fragmentation? Are there ways that your faith community accommodates the fragmentation?

---

1.   Galatians 5:19-21 and elsewhere.
2.   Robert Robinson, "Come, Thou Fount of Every Blessing," *The United Methodist Hymnal* (Nashville: United Methodist Publishing House, 1989), no. 400.

3. As you imagine your faith community becoming more of a self-emptying congregation that helps its members' neighborhoods flourish, what are some of the opportunities for ministry? What are the obstacles to this ministry? How might the congregation move toward overcoming the obstacles? What are the next steps?

4. Jesus prayed that his followers in the future would love one another in the same way that Jesus and the Father love each other. How might Christians who have different theological views find practical ways to become more loving and supportive of one another?

5. Throughout this book we have examined the ways and reasons we can practice the spiritual discipline of celebration throughout the challenges of life. How can our way of being in a divided world cause God to celebrate?

Islands of Sanity

Margaret Wheatley, an expert in organizational behavior and systems change, writes compellingly about what is needed during times of massive systems change within society, which is precisely where we find ourselves today. According to Wheatley, as our society devolves into further fragmentation, violence, and death, what is needed is for people of wisdom and spiritual discernment to form small communities that exist as "islands of sanity" amid the chaos. These islands become beacons of hope and a vision for a better future so that a new society can emerge from the wreckage of the old.

Yet the formation of these islands of sanity, or communities that exist for the sake of others, is not guaranteed. Such communities require a particular type of leadership that is oriented away from what the apostle Paul named as sarx. Such leaders are spiritually attuned, grounded, self-aware, authentic, and willing to pay the price. They are self-differentiated and nonanxious even in the midst of the anxiety of systems change.[3]

Margaret Wheatley, who is not writing from an overtly religious perspective, describes asking this question every time she meets with global leaders to discuss seemingly insurmountable problems in their contexts: "Who do you choose to be for this time? Are you willing to use whatever power and influence you have to create islands of sanity that evoke and rely on our best human qualities to create, produce, and persevere?"[4] These are precisely the questions for us Christians as we consider the call to celebration in the midst of a divided world.

Urban Monastery

I met Maggie Patterson initially through an email. She found me on the internet, she said, and wondered if the Academy for Missional Wisdom (later renamed Launch and Lead) had a training program in Australia or could include people from Australia. She was interested in planting a new faith community that had a new monastic core community, embraced several social and environmental justice foci, and would be an alternative type of

---

3. For an excellent resource on nonanxious, self-differentiated leadership during systems change, see Edwin Friedman, *A Failure of Nerve: Leadership in the Age of the Quick Fix* (New York: Seabury, 2006). A fine little animation that summarizes this book may be found on YouTube: Mathew David Bardwell, "Friedman's Theory of Differentiated Leadership Made Simple," November 10, 2010, https://www.you tube.com/watch?v=RgdcljNV-Ew.

4. Margaret J. Wheatley, *Who Do We Choose to Be? Facing Reality, Claiming Leadership, Restoring Sanity* (Oakland, CA: Berrett-Koehler, 2017), Kindle edition, 11.

church. The questions she asked were exactly the right ones, given her sense of call. Preparation for the particular ministry to which she felt called was beyond the scope of the traditional forms of theological education available to her in her context.

Excited to hear more of her story, I wrote back and asked her to tell me more. I asked if she had any friends in her area who would also be interested in developing the ministry project with her. Before long Maggie responded with one of the most heart-breaking and hopeful stories I have ever heard.[5]

Perhaps a decade before Maggie reached out to me, she and her husband Darryl and their three children lived in a beautiful waterfront home. Maggie was a nurse, and Darryl was a social worker who served vulnerable teens. They had a peaceful life, were committed Christians, had great kids, and enjoyed all the material comforts of a middle-class life. As Darryl told me later, they "were living the Australian dream."

One day after work as they enjoyed a cup of tea, Maggie asked her husband this question: "Darryl, is this life that we have really what Jesus wants for us? Is our own comfort the point of the gospel?" A lively conversation ensued, with both of them coming to the conclusion that not only was their comfortable lifestyle not reflective of the teaching of Jesus with regard to love of suffering neighbors in an economically, racially, and ethnically divided world, it was in fact boring. This conversation was the turning point for their lives.

5. I tell Maggie and Darryl's story with their permission. You can watch a short video interview with Maggie Patterson in which she tells her story, and a video tour of the old orphanage now named Urban Monastery, led by Darryl Patterson, here: "Derelict Orphanage Turned into Place That Serves Vulnerable Children," *Eternity Magazine*, September 1, 2017, https://www.eternitynews.com.au/good-news/derelict-orphanage-turned-into-place-that-serves-vulnerable-children/?fbclid=IwAR3B_CRdgCec5oasWvHrq1Vmk7QJcD5FFLybi-rN6xKeL1qnzWBAL1qX8hU.

Maggie and Darryl agreed to fast and pray and seek God's guidance for next steps. Part of their discernment included reading books by people who had taken up a new monastic way of life, such as Shane Claiborne's *Irresistible Revolution*.[6] Online they studied the history of the Iona Community in Scotland, the Northumbria Community in England, and other Protestant intentional communities that combined worship, justice, and life together that was deeply contextualized. They strategized about how to fund a missional endeavor of this type.

Soon Maggie and Darryl sold their beautiful home and as many of their worldly possessions as they could, resigned from their jobs, moved into a rental property, and opened a bakery in a small tourist village. Their goal was to develop a small business that would generate jobs in the community and in time provide a revenue stream both for their own living and to fund the ministry that would emerge. They began to pray for a building that could house the dream Maggie described in her first email to me.

It took some time for the dream to become reality, in no small part because neither of them had a business background or formal training in running a bakery. But after a few years the bakery broke even financially, then became successful enough to generate the income needed for themselves and their employees and to launch the missional ministry. As they searched for the right property, they found the old, abandoned St. Joseph's Orphanage for girls in Goulburn, New South Wales. The orphanage, they learned, was more expensive than their budget would allow. But they felt sure that it was the right location for the work God had called them to do. By this time their children were young teenagers. The family

---

6. Shane Claiborne, *Irresistible Revolution: Living as an Ordinary Radical* (Grand Rapids: Zondervan, 2006).

decided to go on a pilgrimage to England and Scotland to learn from the Northumbria Community, the Iona Community, and some other communities on Holy Island, Lindisfarne.

While in Glasgow, Maggie and Darryl's daughter Isla became critically ill with a previously undiagnosed heart condition. Her condition rapidly worsened. A heart transplant would be necessary to save her life. In the hours before her surgery, Isla and Darryl made a pact at Isla's insistence that if she didn't make it, the family would continue to live into the dream of the new ministry at the old orphanage. Tragically, Isla did not survive the surgery.

Maggie's first email to me arrived about four months after Isla's death. She and Darryl and their other children had returned to Australia, utterly devastated by the loss of their daughter and sister but committed for Isla's sake to follow through on the dream God had given.

Because the orphanage had suffered significant vandalism while they were in the United Kingdom, the price dropped within range of their budget, and they bought it. A few months after receiving the email in which Maggie shared this story, I went with a colleague from the Missional Wisdom Foundation to Australia to meet Maggie and Darryl and their children and to lead a retreat day with them and dozens of their friends who were eager to see the new ministry come to fruition. We toured the derelict building, which was littered with broken glass, overturned furniture, and rubbish. We prayed together, asking God to strengthen Maggie and Darryl for the important ministry that lay ahead, and we parted with my promise to return.

Over the next five years I returned twice to spend time with Maggie and Darryl to learn from them and for mutual encouragement since my community and I are also pioneering new, multifaceted ministry. This extraordinary couple has lived into the vision that began to present itself to them that day on their porch as they looked out at the beach and wondered what Jesus wanted for their lives. Though it is now called Urban Monastery, it was originally named Liminis House, to indicate the thin veil between heaven and earth where people encounter God in new ways. The massive brick building contains a coffee roastery and a large space for community gatherings, a renovated chapel named for Isla in which people gather daily for morning and evening prayer and where an ecumenical worship gathering takes place on Sunday. Rustic, spacious living quarters house the family. There are two guest cottages for visitors and soon to be completed accommodations in the old dormitories for the regular stream of theology students, church leaders, college students, and others who visit to learn how to neighbor others in the way of Jesus. A courtyard is being brought back to life and will include café tables and chairs, flower boxes, and additional seating. New collaborations are emerging between Urban Monastery and institutions for theological education, including with Neighborhood Seminary.[7]

Maggie has become a self-taught, extremely gifted community organizer who has worked tirelessly with neighbors, business leaders, and civic leaders locally, regionally, and nationally in order to form collaborations that benefit vulnerable women and children and that protect the environment. She has brought together people across economic, racial, ethnic, and theological spectrums to work harmoniously to bring Urban Monastery to fruition. Since the historic building is now being renovated and dedicated to the flourishing of the city, Maggie and Darryl have

7. To find out more about Neighborhood Seminary, see www.neighborhood seminary.org.

found ready support and partnerships from a wide array of non-religious organizations in the city. Most recently, a land developer purchased acreage that surrounds the campus of Urban Monastery and is developing a beautiful planned community called Joseph's Gate. The design of the neighborhood was created in such a way that Urban Monastery could serve as a hub for neighborhood gatherings and could sponsor a large community garden.[8]

The first gathering at Urban Monastery after the initial renovation of the common space was for former residents of St. Joseph's Orphanage. That gathering and subsequent gatherings have provided space, time, and a structured process for people to share their stories. For some participants, these gatherings have been deeply healing, partly because some of their stories included trauma and because the reunions have provided a way for them to reconnect with people who were family-like friends when they lived at St. Joseph's long ago.

Maggie and Darryl and their family will always grieve for Isla, who was probably the biggest champion in the family for the vision of Urban Monastery. But Isla's infectious faith, hope, and love continue to shine through the constellation of emerging ministries at Urban Monastery. Every day that people gather for prayer in Isla's Chapel, every time that a theology class has a field trip at Urban Monastery to learn about new forms of church, every time Maggie brokers meetings between community stakeholders to help the city flourish, there is a divine celebration. God's will is being done on earth as it is in heaven.

In a world fractured by racism, classism, sexism, child trafficking, white nationalism, and more, Urban Monastery has

---

8. See the website for more information as to how the neighborhood will be positioned around Urban Monastery for intentional interaction: https://www.josephs gate.com.au/.

emerged as a house of hospitality, healing, and hope. It is, in fact, an example of what Margaret Wheatley calls an "island of sanity" in a rapidly changing world. For that reason, Urban Monastery already has an impact in this world that is disproportionately large in light of its seemingly small footprint in New South Wales. Emerging forms of faith communities that heal the trauma of individuals, groups, and the environment are lighthouses of divine hope that beckon all of us to celebrate what God wants to do through us.

Questions for Reflection

1. Who do you choose to be at this time for this season?

2. Whose do you choose to be? What are the indicators of your real allegiance?

3. What are the markers that will distinguish you as a person in your location? What are the markers that will distinguish your community of faith in its location?

4. When you think about your community of faith, how does it resonate (or not) with Wheatley's description of an "island of sanity" in a chaotic world? If it does not, what might it take to move toward becoming an "island of sanity"?

5. What are the signs of Christian celebration at Urban Monastery? What are the choices the Pattersons have made in order to foster an "island of sanity" in their own context? What are the core concepts from the work they are doing that could transfer across cultures and neighborhoods?

Loving and Celebrating with Others When We Disagree

From the time of the apostles, Christians have had varieties of interpretations of scripture, theology, politics, and what it means to be engaged in God's mission in the world. Justo González's classic, accessible little volume *Christian Thought Revisited: Three Types of Theology* traces the theological development of three distinctly different streams of thought very early in the history of the church.[9] While there were sharp points of disagreement between ancient Christians in the various traditions—and to be sure, some Christians behaved very badly toward one another at the time—today all three streams are considered to be important tributaries to the broad river of Christian theology. So from the early church we learn that is possible to have different interpretations of scripture and different theological perspectives yet to do so charitably, without demonizing or damning those with whom we disagree.[10]

It is not just possible but utterly necessary in our day to form genuinely loving and respectful relationships with those with whom we disagree. If we do not learn to do this well, we will have no authority with which to speak to our neighbors about God. All our God talk will do is further the fragmentation of our culture. We cannot with integrity celebrate the love of God who is making all things new while we posture, label, judge, reject, vilify, and harm other Christians. Much less can we justify hateful words and

---

9.   Justo González, *Christian Thought Revisited* (Maryknoll, NY: Orbis, 2013).

10.   Writing in 2009, Brian McLaren makes a compelling argument through a reflection on the many Jesuses of different Christian traditions. His book was instantly controversial among conservative Christians because of his irenic posture toward all Christian traditions. Brian McLaren, *A Generous Orthodoxy* (Grand Rapids: Zondervan, 2009).

deeds against people of other religions or no religion, as if we were doing God a favor.

This is not a liberal or conservative matter. Love of neighbor is a central fact of Jesus's life and teaching. We worship a God who sends rain on the just and the unjust, Jesus says in Matthew 5:45. We must exercise the same kind of generosity if we want to be the children of God. Love for neighbor requires compassion, regardless of that neighbor's theology. Love for enemy—our most despised neighbor—is at the heart of the gospel. To avoid or excise this fact from our practice of the Christian life out of doctrinal preservation or theological idealism is to commit violence against Jesus and his teaching. Learning to love our enemies is pivotal to becoming the answer to Jesus's prayer of John 17, that we may be one as the Father and Jesus are one. Love of enemy is the epicenter of the Gospels.

Loving Cornelius

So here's the thing. The simple fact of Cornelius was unthinkable for Peter. He could not imagine a Cornelius culturally, politically, or religiously. Nothing in his life thus far had prepared him for the encounter. He knew what a centurion was, of course. Being a first-century Jew in Roman-occupied Palestine had taught him all about centurions. These were officers with at least a hundred and often two hundred soldiers under their command. Centurions had to be steadfast, faithful, and fearless because they led their men into battle from the front line. Peter knew all of that intellectually.

But there were other things about centurions that Peter knew viscerally, that his body knew, memories so ghastly and so traumatic that words could never capture the horror he experienced from a centurion. All he had to do was hear the word *centurion* and Peter was there, back at Golgotha watching Jesus's life drain away while soldiers played a game. The winner got to keep Jesus's clothes. Just the sight of a crested helmet bobbing through the marketplace was enough. He could hear his own voice telling the girl in the courtyard, "I never knew him."

Peter's worst nightmare was a centurion. His deepest shame was linked to Roman soldiers. Even with Jewish purity laws that labeled all sorts of people temporarily or permanently unclean, there could be no person more abhorrent or more evil in Peter's imagination than a centurion. Centurions were, for Peter, evil incarnate.

So it was that Cornelius was beyond Peter's capacity to imagine. A centurion who worshiped the same God Peter worshiped? Impossible! A centurion who was a contemplative, who spent time every day in attentiveness to God, open to God's direction? Absurd! A centurion who gave instead of took from the poor? A centurion who was a mystic, who could see and hear angels? One who would humble himself to seek wisdom from a tanner's house where the clothing, skin, and hair of everyone in that house reeked of the urine and feces used to tan the hides?

Cornelius was absolutely beyond Peter's imagination.

So it was that our God, who is often a healing trickster, gave Peter the vision of something like a sheet coming down from heaven. I wonder if it was a tablecloth? Notice how God came to Peter through his bodily hunger. Notice how God breaks our theological rules, the ones contained in Holy Scripture. Three times the Lord spoke to Peter with this vision, telling him to eat that which is forbidden by the Bible. The Lord concluded a final time with, "What God has made clean, you must not call profane" (Acts 10:15).

Peter recognized the voice as the Lord, a voice he knew and loved, a voice he trusted, but what was going on? And in that space, the ambassage arrived from Cornelius, a centurion. There was so much more at stake here than Peter could know. God was absolutely invested in answering Cornelius's prayers. God had no trouble imagining Cornelius, whom Peter thought of as worse than an outsider, as already being part of God's family. This story is deeply troubling to our certitude about who's in and who's out, who's good and who's bad. Our dualistic categories cannot hold this story.

The salvation of the whole world, not just a handful of Jews, was unfolding. God's intent was so far beyond what Peter could imagine. And that intent included healing Peter of the deep trauma inflicted upon him by a centurion and everything that centurions represented. Salvation—forgiveness of sin, healing of wounds, liberation from bondage, a new creation—was coming to Peter anew, *through the centurion*.

In Peter's case, the healing was going to involve a despised other—the centurion—falling at Peter's feet in awe and wonder, a centurion who was utterly undone by God's movement in his life. As Peter saw this man in humility and vulnerability on the floor before him, a crack opened in the hard shell around Peter's memories, Peter's horror, Peter's shame—and a tiny seed of solidarity took root.

"Get up," he said to Cornelius, "I am only a man." What he meant was, "I am a man *like you*." So yes, this is the story of Peter taking the gospel to Gentiles, Peter moving beyond the boundary between Jew and Gentile in the early history of the church. But this story is so much more than that. It is a story of the mystery of reconciliation, the wonder of how God works to heal our own grief as we reach beyond our fear and our painful memories and our stunted imagination to offer genuine hospitality to others.

This is the story that we must now inhabit if we are going to follow Jesus. For we are in a day in which the gospel is publicly conflated with religious violence, with political gimmickry, with racism and homophobia, with xenophobia. Our neighbors hear the religious voices that hate in the name of God. They need to see us living this story, the true story of what kind of God, God is.

But within the church we keep circling around like people trapped in a labyrinth. We know God wants us to reach beyond our walls, we know that the world is rapidly changing and that we must change how we are present to the world, but we are filled with fear over losing our identity if we even allow ourselves to think that outsiders just might know God without us. It is disorienting and disturbing to think that outsiders might pray and God might hear their prayers, that outsiders might have spiritual experiences that are from the same God we worship, that they might be more motivated than we are to tend the poor and suffering in our cities, that outsiders might actually hear and respond to God in breathtaking humility and vulnerability.

And it's not just any outsiders but outsiders from the very groups that we are sure are profane. The people we think we get to hate. Salvation is coming to us through "the other" in ways that can only come through them, to heal our many wounds and to open our hearts to the love of God that knows no limit.[11]

---

11. This section focusing on Cornelius is drawn from a sermon I preached for Opening Convocation at Duke Chapel, August 30, 2016, when I was installed as Dean of the Divinity School.

Questions for Reflection

1. What did Cornelius need from Peter? What was it about Peter that God might have particularly used to open Cornelius to new dimensions of God's love?

2. As you think about the story of Cornelius as a member of a despised people group (centurions), who are the despised people groups in our culture? First, think in terms of which groups are despised by the dominant culture. Then name the despised groups from the standpoint of your own religious culture. How is contempt shown to the despised groups? What are some of the social, spiritual, and relational outcomes of that contempt?

3. What might it look like within your social context to welcome God who comes to us through the despised group? How could that be facilitated? What are the major obstacles that would need to be negotiated in order to open yourself and your community to welcoming and celebrating God who comes through "the other"?

For the remainder of this chapter we will consider some examples of the crucial challenge we now face in celebrating God's love in the midst of a divided world. Each of these examples has changed my understanding of what it means to follow a God who sends rain on the just and the unjust, a God who is most easily found among "the least of these." Not only have these experiences changed what I believe, but they have changed how I live. For after all, we do live what we actually believe, regardless of what we say during a liturgy.

Love the Sinner, Hate the Sin?

When she was in junior high, my sister Jeanine came to faith in the Southern Baptist church.[12] She was eager to help our parents find Jesus because Lord knows, they had their troubles. I was just as determined in my Pentecostal zeal, so between the two of us we made sure that Mom and Dad understood the perils of hell that awaited them should they not repent. Amazingly, they did come to faith years later, in spite of us.

Jeanine was an evangelist through and through. She went to church twice on Sundays and once in the middle of the week, read her Bible, went to youth events, and did everything that was asked of her, with gusto. A few years later she left the Southern Baptist church to embrace a very rigorous form of orthodoxy, where her life and faith were exemplary as she raised her family and attended to the many liturgical requirements of her tradition. Theological certitude was her way of life, until it wasn't. The day finally came when Jeanine looked into the mirror and told herself the truth about herself. She could no longer present to the world an illusion of her identity that deeply conflicted with who she really is. As is the case for many people, this happened as she moved from young adulthood to middle age.

Jeanine tells me that she never really understood what Jesus meant by turning the other cheek until she came out. She says she never really had to show grace—unmerited favor and regard—toward people who hate her until she discovered she was suddenly

12. My sister, Jeanine Heath-McGlinn has given me permission to tell this part of her story. We write in our joint memoir about growing up in our violent, chaotic family and then gradually moving into our healing vocations in our forthcoming book, *Loving the Hell Out of Ourselves*. Jeanine is a therapist, and we sometimes lead healing retreats, workshops, and seminars together.

the despised "other" and now had droves of Christian haters. In her religious context, Jeanine suddenly embodied everything her coreligionists feared and hated. What did the hating look like? Excommunication. Bullying. Religious double-speak such as, "We love you unconditionally, but ..." There were written threats to her health and safety. Ugly stares. Harassment. Over many subsequent years having to hear her long-term, monogamous relationship and beloved wife, also a Christian, described as an abomination, and worse, all "in the name of Jesus." Coming out in an exclusive, shaming Christian world is the very means by which she had to wrestle with and choose, over and over, the prayer of Jesus: "Forgive them; for they know not what they do" (Luke 23:34 KJV).

As for myself, I attended a somewhat progressive evangelical seminary in the early 1990s. While women and minorities were welcomed and honored at my institution, members of the LGBTQ community were not. The methods of biblical interpretation that I learned were beautiful in many ways but inadequate when it came to human sexuality.

When Jeanine came out, I had only recently graduated from seminary and had yet to do any significant theological work in the area of sexuality, other than in the area of sexual abuse. On that subject I had considerable knowledge, theoretically, pastorally, and personally. Jeanine asked what my beliefs were about her newly disclosed identity, whether I thought she was sinful for being gay. I didn't know what to say. The method of biblical interpretation that I learned in seminary told me that being gay is a sin. But I experienced Jeanine as a loving, virtuous, worshipful, Christlike person whose life truly makes the world a better place. So I said to her, "I'm going to have to learn about other perspectives on the Scriptures that are used to forbid your relationship. The interpretive method I learned in seminary tells me you are sinful for being gay, but it doesn't make sense. I know you! Let me work on this and come back to you about it. Regardless of what my beliefs are, I love you dearly and will not tolerate anyone hurting you."

That was the beginning of a slow process that resulted in changing my mind about fully welcoming and including LGBTQ persons in the life of the church. Over time, with much study and reflection not only on biblical interpretation but in hearing the stories of suffering inflicted against LGBTQ people by Christians, I came to a much more Christ-centered theology of inclusion.[13]

We have talked about the irony of this turn of events a lot over the years, partly because I am a theologian and Jeanine is a therapist. We know from our own journeys and from our work in tending hearts and souls that what passes as a theology of human sexuality in most churches is woefully incomplete and often just plain wrong. The problem, we think, is that the wrong set of questions and binary thinking shape the discussion:

- Are you homo (bad) or hetero (good)?
- Is your sexuality a chosen lifestyle (homo) or the way you were born and part of being human (hetero)?
- Are you fornicating (bad) or having sex with your spouse (good)?
- Are you married (good) or single (highly suspect)?

---

13.   For a profound family story about a daughter who came out, from one of the best known and beloved bishops of The United Methodist Church, see "Bishop Richard Wilke: A Plea to The United Methodist Church," Ministry Matters, https://www .ministrymatters.com/all/entry/9760/bishop-richard-wilke-a-plea-to-the-united -methodist-church, August 19, 2019. Bishop Wilke is the author of the Disciple Bible Studies, which have been used by millions of Christians around the world to foster deep devotion to Christ and an active life of discipleship for the transformation of the world.

These questions and others like them are too simplistic and too dualistic. They assume too much and ask too little. They do not interface with what we know from science or the lived experience of countless LGBTQ persons.

It is time for the church to ask new, better questions about sexuality, sexual virtue, and sexual vice. Jeanine and I think the springboard for the new questions is not *sexual expression* or affectional orientation, but *imago Dei*, the inherent sanctity and dignity of human life. The *homo* that has our attention is *Homo sapiens*, what it means to be human beings. Do we Christians understand ourselves and others first and foremost as full-orbed human beings made in the image of God? The question of sexual orientation that concerns Jeanine and me is not whether people are *hetero* but are *vehemens*, having an orientation toward violence.

To reference themes of the previous chapter, these questions that Jeanine and I have pondered have emerged from the humus of our earlier theological failure regarding human sexuality. What we thought we knew about God early in our formation as zealots was well intentioned but incorrect. We said many words about God, but then through life's cataclysms, we encountered God in ways that rendered us mute, sitting in the dust in the presence of God.

Jeanine tells a story of how one night she was looking out at the lake through the birch trees. The cloudless night was luminous, signaling that the moon must be out, but she could not see the moon. Then she moved slightly to one side and saw the rising moon, which had been obscured by a tree. There are many things in life, Jeanine says, that become trees hiding the moon. Although the reality of something is right there in front of us, we cannot see it. As long as we are rigid, as long as we fear losing an argument more than we fear harming others, we will not see it. But if we will open ourselves to learn from different perspectives, if we will approach others whose views on an issue are at odds with our own, in a posture of curiosity and humility, we will see what was "hidden in plain sight." Then, even if we continue to hold a different view, we can do so while remaining in loving relationship with others.

Civility and Celebration in a Divided World

One of the toughest challenges facing our society today is loss of capacity for civil discourse over matters that concern our nation. An example of this problem is lack of civility in our institutes of higher education, on college campuses, even in graduate schools and yes, sadly, even in theological seminaries. What is civility? Does civility, as its detractors claim, hamper intellectual freedom? Quite the opposite. Civility is the ability to engage in lively, vigorous debate in which people interrogate a range of perspectives about any number of issues while maintaining a respectful climate in which the discussion takes place, whether in real time and physical space or digitally. Civility rejects demonizing those with whom we disagree. Civility refuses the cowardly and cruel practices of bullying, online character assassination, undermining others' credibility with narrative "spin." Civility eschews the use of innuendo, threat, manipulation, and other tactics that are all too common among knowledge workers in shame-based departments and schools.

Today on campuses, individuals and groups act out hostilities against one another in ways that would have been unthinkable a few years ago. *The Chronicle of Higher Education*, the leading professional journal for people who work in higher education, has published dozens of articles in recent years on topics such as faculty incivility; faculty bullying of colleagues and students; administrators and faculty who were harassed and driven from their posts because of clashes between student expectations of safety over against freedom of speech by invited lecturers; academic freedom used as an excuse by tenured faculty for creating a hostile work environment against untenured, minority, or female colleagues; students demanding to have trigger warnings before lectures and designated safe spaces where they will not be challenged by others with opposing views.[14]

Restoring the art of civility will be essential in order to save educational institutions from self-destruction. Without skill in civility, future leaders will not be able to lead negotiations toward justice and peace. The world will become increasingly violent. Thus one of the most pressing questions for those of us who are leading innovation in higher education is how to model and teach the art of civility in the core curricula.

Writing for *Edutopia*, Daniel Levitin describes an innovative new program, Minerva Schools, at the Keck Graduate Institute of Claremont Colleges. "Preparing to succeed in an era of uncertainty requires developing your intellect, building your character, and learning practical capabilities," states the banner on the school's website.[15] At Minerva Schools the learning experience is

14. For just a small sampling see Karin Fischer, "College Founded by Yale and National U. of Singapore Cancels Program on Dissent," *The Chronicle of Higher Education*, September 18, 2019; Megan Zahneis, "I Don't Think We Should Be Afraid of Protests: Marquette Faculty Members Speak Out Against Policy Requiring Approval for Demonstrations," *The Chronicle of Higher Education*, August 29, 2019; and Terry Nguyen, "I Was Sick to My Stomach: A Scholar's Bullying Reputation Goes under the Microscope," *The Chronicle of Higher Education*, May 30, 2019.

15. https://www.minerva.kgi.edu/.

designed to produce leaders who practice civility as a way of life explicitly to make the world a better place:

> So that they can succeed in this interconnected world, we teach our students to develop a sensitivity to different cultural norms as well as an ability to work with people from very different backgrounds, with varying viewpoints and experiences. Much of this is woven into the fabric of our student body; our students come from more than 60 countries and a wide range of socioeconomic, ethnic, political, and religious backgrounds. Through these experiences, Minerva students learn to evaluate the ethical and moral consequences of their decisions and to try to make the world a better place for the sake of doing so—not because they might get recognition.[16]

Beyond emerging innovation within academia, programs that foster positive social change such as The People's Supper are gaining traction even as society spirals into worse chaos and fragmentation. The People's Supper is a structured dinner with conversation that reminds me of table fellowship as practiced by Jesus. By gathering people with radically different backgrounds, views, political commitments, races, sexual orientations, and religions around a dinner table with carefully developed conversation practices, The People's Supper teaches practices of hospitality, deep listening, and nonviolence. It helps people form genuine relationships while breaking bread. "Social change moves at the speed of relationships. Relationships move at the speed of trust," states the banner on their website.[17] While not an overtly religious organization, The People's Supper programs are being used increasingly by congregations, theology schools, and other religious organizations

---

16. Daniel Levitin, "A New Model of Higher Education," *Edutopia*, June 22, 2018, https://www.edutopia.org/article/new-model-higher-education.

17. https://thepeoplessupper.org/.

in order to reclaim their forgotten practices of deep listening, genuine hospitality, and speaking from a heart of love.

The New Creation

As we move further into the twenty-first century, the kind of miracle that will draw postreligious, nonreligious, and antireligious people into a life-giving relationship with God will be signs and wonders of reconciliation. Our neighbors need to see, in the church and in our neighborhoods, intentional processes of reconciliation specifically between all the groups in which toxic religion has fueled hate and violence. To put it bluntly, our neighbors need to experience love in action, from us, for their sake. It is time for us to be filled with the Spirit of Christ, which will then "[become] flesh and blood, and [move] into the neighborhood," as *The Message* states in John 1:14.

Explaining what kind of attitudes and actions will create this kind of future, the apostle Paul wrote these words:

> From now on, therefore, we regard no one from a human point of view; even though we once knew Christ from a human point of view, we know him no longer in that way. So if anyone is in Christ, there is a new creation: everything old has passed away; see, everything has become new! All this is from God, who reconciled us to himself through Christ, and has given us the ministry of reconciliation; that is, in Christ God was reconciling the world to himself, not counting their trespasses against them, and entrusting the message of reconciliation to us. So we are ambassadors for Christ, since God is making his appeal through us; we entreat you on behalf of Christ, be reconciled to God. (2 Corinthians 5:16-20)

This is the ultimate form of celebration for followers of Jesus—to serve as ambassadors of reconciliation, to be full participants in God's mighty work of making all things new. Every thought, word, and deed that opens ourselves and others to God's reconciling, re-creating love pushes back the powers and principalities, sings the dead to life, and drives gloom away with glad tidings of great joy.

So it is that our anthem of celebration echoes the joyous words of Isaiah 61:10-11:

> I will greatly rejoice in the LORD,
> > my whole being shall exult in my God;
> for he has clothed me with the garments of salvation,
> > he has covered me with the robe of righteousness,
> as a bridegroom decks himself with a garland,
> > and as a bride adorns herself with her jewels.
> For as the earth brings forth its shoots,
> > and as a garden causes what is sown in it to spring up,
> so the Lord GOD will cause righteousness and praise
> > to spring up before all the nations.

Questions for Reflection

1. How have you experienced or witnessed polarization in your own social context? How, if at all, has it affected your faith community?

2. When you think about eating dinner with people with whom you have strong disagreements about religion, politics, or morality, what do you feel? What do you imagine would happen?

3. Think about the binary labels *conservative* and *liberal*. How do these labels limit ourselves and others and contribute to incivility?

4. What might be good ground rules for a discussion in which people hold very different views yet conduct themselves with civility?

5. How does the practice of civility lead to celebration?

6. What is the relationship between civility and love of neighbor?